S. Hrg. 114–74

AMERICAN FOOD AID: WHY REFORM MATTERS

HEARING

BEFORE THE

COMMITTEE ON FOREIGN RELATIONS
UNITED STATES SENATE

ONE HUNDRED FOURTEENTH CONGRESS

FIRST SESSION

APRIL 15, 2015

Printed for the use of the Committee on Foreign Relations

Available via the World Wide Web: http://www.gpo.gov/fdsys/

U.S. GOVERNMENT PUBLISHING OFFICE

96–849 PDF   WASHINGTON : 2015

For sale by the Superintendent of Documents, U.S. Government Publishing Office
Internet: bookstore.gpo.gov   Phone: toll free (866) 512–1800; DC area (202) 512–1800
Fax: (202) 512–2104   Mail: Stop IDCC, Washington, DC 20402–0001

(II)

CONTENTS

AMERICAN FOOD AID:
WHY REFORM MATTERS

WEDNESDAY, APRIL 15, 2015

U.S. SENATE,
COMMITTEE ON FOREIGN RELATIONS,
Washington, DC.

The committee met, pursuant to notice, at 9:33 a.m., in room SD–419, Dirksen Senate Office Building, Hon. Bob Corker (chairman of the committee) presiding.

Present: Senator Corker, Gardner, Perdue, Cardin, Shaheen, Coons, Murphy, and Kaine.

OPENING STATEMENT OF HON. BOB CORKER,
U.S. SENATOR FROM TENNESSEE

The CHAIRMAN. The Foreign Relations Committee will come to order.

I want to welcome our witness. I understand there may be circumstances where you may need to depart. We are just glad you are here. If you need to leave in 2 minutes, leave. I understand that there may be something occurring that will cause that. So please, just whatever makes you comfortable.

I am glad to be here with our outstanding ranking member, who I have enjoyed working with so much. And I am glad we are having this hearing today on something that is so important to people around the world.

I do not normally read opening statements. I think I may do it. We have been sort of focused on another issue for a while, but I think people know that since 1954, U.S. international food aid programs have helped to feed over 3 billion people and promote food security in over 150 countries. Most U.S. food aid is provided through Food for Peace, which is currently funded, on average, at $1.6 billion annually. Over the past 5 years, U.S. food aid has helped 56 million people, on average, per year.

Today's hearing will provide the committee with an update on the current operations of the program, including the challenges it faces while responding to increasingly dangerous emergencies.

This increasingly challenging global environment has illustrated to Congress the need for greater flexibility in how Food for Peace operates. The law requires that 100 percent of the food aid to be delivered be U.S.-purchased commodities, and 50 percent of that is to be shipped on U.S.-flagged vessels.

While recent reforms in the farm bill provide some administrative funds to be used for such things as locally and regionally purchased food aid and/or food vouchers, this limited flexibility must be executed in tandem with U.S.-purchased commodities. The cargo and commodity preferences create inefficiencies that undermine our ability to get maximum impact in addressing poverty and suffering from our U.S. food aid dollars.

In some cases, where U.S. national security interests are at stake, like in Syria and other regions in conflict, U.S. food aid plays an important role in U.S. policy and engagement. These interventions would not be possible if we relied on U.S.-purchased commodities.

Increasing flexibility in the Food for Peace program would provide up to $444 million in savings, allowing the United States to reach as many as 12 million more starving people, up to 2½ months faster in some cases.

Again, I think this just jumps out at us, that self-imposed limitations—I am tired, I have not had a lot of sleep. I will just say that the special interests that capture this program cause people around the world to starve.

While the impact of reforming U.S. food aid overseas is profound, the domestic implications are minor, as food aid only contributes 1.41 percent to net farm income and 0.86 percent to agriculture exports.

I have joined forces with my friend and colleague, Senator Coons, by authorizing with him the Food for Peace Reform Act. We are seeking to increase the flexibility of our food aid programs and are looking to our witnesses today to illustrate why reform to the program matters.

For many around the globe we are not yet reaching but could, it is a matter of life and death.

Again, we thank you for being here. I look forward to turning to Senator Cardin and maybe Senator Coons, who has been such a champion.

But I hope that out of this hearing, something is going to occur where we will do the things necessary to make sure that our U.S. dollars help those people that today, as we sit here in this comfort, are starving because of special interests here in our own Nation.

With that, Senator Cardin.

OPENING STATEMENT OF THE HON. BENJAMIN L. CARDIN, U.S. SENATOR FROM MARYLAND

Senator CARDIN. Senator Corker, first of all, thank you for convening this hearing.

Yesterday, this committee dealt with a very visible issue of national security, and that is preventing Iran from becoming a nuclear weapon state. Today, we are dealing with another issue of national security, but it is not quite as visible as the possibility of a nuclear Iran.

I think we all understand that extremists get their strength from people who are desperate and have little hope. And when you are hungry, you are desperate.

So this is an issue, as I see it, of national security. It also, of course, is an issue of what this country stands for, the values of America, what this country has been, a leader worldwide in promoting the right values.

So I welcome this hearing. I thank Senator Corker, I thank Senator Coons, for their leadership in bringing forward reform of our food aid and the Food for Peace program so that we can do more with the resources that we have.

Senator Corker pointed out the incredible record that this country has had since 1954. Three billion people have benefited from U.S. programs in 150 countries. That is an incredible record.

But let me give you one that we are not proud about. Since 2009, the Food for Peace program has lost about 37 percent of its funding, in spite of the fact that the international need has grown. Today, 805 million people are estimated to be chronically hungry; and 51.2 million people have been displaced by conflict. So the needs today are greater, and the resources are less.

The United States has provided international leadership. Because I represent the Senate at the United Nations, along with Senator Johnson, I have had the opportunity to be up at the United Nations to talk about the millennium development goals and discuss where we have been successful. But to get people out of poverty and hunger is an international effort.

These millennium development goals are working. But U.S. leadership is critically important.

So we have to do a better job with Food for Peace. And the legislation that the two of you have brought forward is about using our money more efficiently. It has been estimated that we could serve as many as 8 million to 12 million more people with the same amount of resources, if we reform the system—8 million to 12 million. I know numbers. You do not see numbers. You could have all those people here today. I think it would be a very visible reminder that we have to do a better job, and it really could have a major impact on our goals and on our national security.

I do want to give a word of caution. There are serious issues that have to be resolved, if we are going to be able to move this legislation forward. We have concerns in the maritime industry. We have concerns with U.S. agriculture. We have concerns by the partnerships with our NGOs, dealing with lockbox and monetization and other issues. These are legitimate concerns, and we are going to have to work through that.

But, Mr. Chairman, if we can work through the nuclear review agreement, this should be a piece of cake. We should be able to get this done.

So I look forward to hearing from our witnesses. I would ask unanimous consent that I can put statements in the record from Catholic Relief Services, which is headquartered in Baltimore, MD; the U.S. Maritime Industry; and Bread for the World.

The CHAIRMAN. Without objection.

[EDITOR'S NOTE.—The statements mentioned above can be found in the "Additional Material Submitted for the Record" section at the end of this hearing.]

The CHAIRMAN. I am glad that these entities that have so much to do with this program will have a chance. I know we tried to accommodate additional witnesses. But anyway, I am glad you made that statement.

I wonder if Senator Coons would like to make an opening comment.

STATEMENT OF HON. CHRISTOPHER A. COONS, U.S. SENATOR FROM DELAWARE

Senator COONS. Thank you, Chairman Corker. I will be brief.

I just want to thank Ranking Member Cardin and you, Chairman Corker, for continuing to bring forward a spirit of bipartisanship and a focus on important and difficult issues.

Out of yesterday's markup, I continue to be optimistic we can tackle all sorts of big challenges.

Food aid reform is one that has eluded any significant progress for a long time. As you have both cited, it has made enormous impacts around the world. It has fed billions of people over decades.

But the twin challenges we face are how to make this program more efficient so that it reaches more people, so that it does the best we can with taxpayer dollars. Yet how do we sustain food aid so that we do not, by making changes that pursue efficiency, suddenly wake up and realize we have lost half or two-thirds of the funding, and in reaching to feed 8 million to 12 million more, ultimately end up feeding fewer? That is the political Rubik's Cube that we need to work together to solve.

There is no doubt. There have been studies from GAO to George Mason to nonprofit groups. There is no doubt the current system is inefficient, and it wastes a significant amount both of the commodity and costs. But the core question is, Can we make it both more efficient and more sustainable? I really look forward to working with both of you to achieve that goal.

Thank you for this hearing today.

The CHAIRMAN. Thank you. And I think people should know, for the record, one of the reasons that we are having this hearing today is a commitment that was made to Senator Coons, as we closed out last year, that we would deal with this issue. So I thank him for his leadership.

Our first witness is director Dina Esposito, as long as she is here, from the USAID Office of Food for Peace. Director Esposito manages the Food for Peace program, which responds to acute food insecurity by providing in-kind food aid locally and regionally procured food aid, food vouchers, and cash transfers to millions of people affected by conflict and natural disasters annually.

In addition, it also supports interventions in critical areas such as nutrition, health, agriculture, and livelihood to address the underlying causes of poverty and hunger among the poorest of the poor with development food aid.

Thank you for being here and sharing your thoughts. Please take however long you wish to share those thoughts. Then we will have questions. Thank you very much.

STATEMENT OF DINA ESPOSITO, DIRECTOR OF THE OFFICE OF FOOD FOR PEACE, UNITED STATES AGENCY FOR INTERNATIONAL DEVELOPMENT, WASHINGTON, DC

Ms. ESPOSITO. Chairman Corker, Ranking Member Cardin, and distinguished members of the committee, thank you for inviting me today to testify on the administration's efforts to modernize and improve the U.S. food aid programs. We appreciate the opportunity to share how USAID's Office of Food for Peace is working to make our food assistance programs more efficient and effective in a changing world.

We likewise recognize and appreciate your bipartisan interest in modernizing food assistance as expressed in your recently introduced Food for Peace Reform Act.

I first started in humanitarian aid work back in the early 1990s. At that time, I had the opportunity to visit with refugees and displaced persons in many hotspots around the world. Today, as the Food for Peace director, I am still visiting troubled spots.

While the circumstances are equally tragic, and our commitment just as constant, I am struck by just how different our response options now are. Expanding markets, new technologies, and other innovations make the world a different place.

But these opportunities are accompanied by new challenges. Today, more people are affected by conflict and natural disasters than any time since World War II. And the cost of traditional food aid is rising, making it increasingly difficult to meet even minimum levels of global need.

Given these factors, and an overall constrained budget environment, further reforming U.S. food aid programs to advance our humanitarian, economic, and national security interests make sense. Our reform proposals build on a clear evidence base of the last 5 years, as well as bipartisan efforts, dating from President Bush's initial calls for reform after the food price crisis in 2008. Those calls laid the groundwork for Food for Peace's emergency food security program. This initiative established in 2010 through the international disaster assistance account supports local and regional procurement and targeted cash and voucher-based food assistance.

Our data confirms the analysis undertaken by the Government Accountability Office that food purchased locally and regionally is more cost-efficient. For Africa, it is, on average, 34 percent more efficient than shipping food aid from the United States. Response time is also faster. U.S. in-kind food commodities can take 4 to 6 months to reach beneficiaries while food purchased closer to those in need can cut that time in half.

I want to provide two real-world examples of how flexibility in our food assistance programs is making a difference. More than 10 million Syrians are displaced today, and 4 million are refugees in neighboring countries, including Lebanon and Jordan. Most do not live in camps. They live in the towns and cities of these middle-income countries where commerce is active and grocery stores accessible.

To address this vast and complex crisis, donors, led by the United States, are supporting a food assistance debit card so refugees can buy food in local markets. The debit card not only provides greater choice and dignity to those war victims but, as importantly, eases the pressure on host communities by supporting local merchants and adding jobs through expanded businesses. Meeting life-saving needs in this way contributes to the stability of U.S. allies in this troubled region.

After a natural disaster, responding rapidly can mean the difference between life and death. Following Hurricane Haiyan in the Philippines, we responded with the purchase of local food stocks that reached storm victims within days of the event. Six weeks later, U.S. food commodities prepositioned in the region arrived, followed by more food from the United States.

Growing our ability to always respond with the right tool at the right time led to the administration's fiscal year 2014 food aid reform proposal. While the proposed reforms were not adopted, the 2014 farm bill did give Food for Peace 7 percent increased flexibility. This reform alone helped us to reach some 600,000 additional beneficiaries last year. But we could do so much more.

Food for Peace regularly finds opportunities to improve efficiencies. Just recently, we saved $4 million in the Democratic Republic of Congo by buying food locally as part of our relief response. With greater flexibility, we would have purchased even more locally, generating an additional $12 million in savings.

Missed opportunities like these are why the President's fiscal year 2016 budget once again includes a request for reform of food aid programs.

I must emphasize that reform does not equal no U.S. in-kind food. Last year, for example, the United States provided 120,000 tons of U.S. food to South Sudan when conflict cut off millions and markets were not functioning, pulling that country back from the brink of famine. This was the right tool at the right time, which is what food aid reform is all about.

I would be remiss if I did not close by saying that we at the USAID Office of Food for Peace are proud to be managing the resources so generously provided by the American people to alleviate hunger and suffering overseas.

I also want to recognize our many stakeholders who make this work possible and honor those who risk their lives to deliver assistance to hungry people around the world.

Thank you again for your continued commitment to ending global hunger. I look forward to your questions.

[The prepared statement of Ms. Esposito follows:]

PREPARED STATEMENT OF DINA ESPOSITO

INTRODUCTION

Chairman Corker, Ranking Member Cardin, and distinguished members of the committee, thank you for inviting me today to testify on the United States Agency for International Development's (USAID) efforts to modernize and improve U.S. food aid programs. We appreciate the opportunity to share how USAID's Office of Food for Peace (FFP) is working to make our food assistance programs more efficient and effective in a changing world. We likewise recognize and appreciate your bipartisan interest, as expressed in the recently introduced Food for Peace Reform Act, to see food aid modernized.

I first started in humanitarian aid work in 1989 and in the early 1990s I had the opportunity to visit with refugees and displaced persons in many hotspots around the world, including in places like Liberia, Mozambique, South Sudan, and Somalia. Today as the USAID/FFP Director I am still visiting trouble spots and while the circumstances are equally tragic, I am always struck by just how different the response options available to us are—the use of electronic food vouchers and mobile money to deliver assistance, new technology to better identify beneficiaries, satellite imagery to confirm public works projects are completed—the world is a different place.

USAID is the largest provider of food assistance in the world and we are seeking to maintain our leadership role—to be the best at what we do—by evolving our programs with the times. So today I would like to share with you the evolution of food aid and how evidenced-based learning can improve our programs. I also want to highlight how we are currently using the flexibility provided through the International Disaster Assistance account and how the critical reforms in the 2014 farm bill are enabling USAID to reach more people quickly and cost-effectively. These reforms serve as the basis for USAID to continue to pursue additional flexibility in food crises to use the right tool at the right time.

LOOKING BACK, LOOKING FORWARD

In 1954, President Eisenhower created the Food for Peace program to ship surplus U.S. food to the developing world and to countries still recovering from World War II. For over 60 years, the Food for Peace Title II program has allowed the United States to live up to its historic mission to alleviate hunger around the world. Through the generosity of the American people we have fed billions of the world's neediest people—perhaps the largest and longest running expression of humanity ever seen. This has been—and continues to be—possible through the incredible partnership with American farmers, implementing partners, maritime industry partners, and Congress. While we look back on these American achievements with pride, we must also recognize that the world has changed. New opportunities and challenges are presented to us.

Some of the countries that have received title II U.S. food and other foreign assistance, such as the Republic of Korea, have developed strong economies and become important U.S. trade partners. Foreign direct investment now exceeds development assistance in many of the poorest regions of the world and there is steady economic growth in remote parts of the globe, including in many places where we have historically shipped United States food aid. People can now use cell phones to receive emergency transfers and humanitarian workers can access local banks and food markets to buy and transfer aid to those in need in a way that fosters greater local economic activity and may help to reduce the severity of food crises and their underlying causes.

At the African Union Summit in June, African leaders committed to ending hunger and halving poverty on their continent by 2025 and building resilience to climate-related events, like droughts. USAID/Food for Peace's programs support the United States Government's lead initiative in this area, Feed the Future. As part of this effort, USAID's programs seek to decrease hunger by increasing both agricultural production and the incomes of smallholder women and men in areas with high malnutrition and poverty rates who rely on this sector for their livelihoods.

Rising costs and growing needs

Within the changing global landscape, the role of United States in-kind commodity food aid is changing. Strong commercial demand for United States food means that commercial exports have risen dramatically. And food aid has declined as an overall share of United States food exports, representing less than one-half of one percent of the total value today and an even smaller share of overall U.S. agricultural production. USAID shipped over 3 million tons of in-kind aid in 2003, as compared to just over 1 million last year—in large part due to the rising costs of delivering food aid and the complex nature of many food security crises.

While we are getting less for our dollar with United States in-kind food assistance the need for emergency food assistance is higher than ever as a record number of civil conflicts and natural disasters continue to threaten the livelihoods of the poorest men, women, and children around the globe.

The U.N. High Commissioner for Refugees reported last year that more than 51 million people are displaced today by conflict—more than at any time since World War II. The numbers are staggering—for every one person who returned home last year, four more were displaced; 3 million new refugees fled their countries in the last 3 years—half of them children; and there are now 33 million conflict-affected people still inside their home borders—more than 5 million of them displaced in just the last few years. The places generating these grim statistics are familiar to you— Syria, Iraq, South Sudan, the Central African Republic, Somalia, to name a few.

Coupled with these conflict drivers of hunger, the increasing frequency and volatility of extreme weather events, slow or stagnant economic growth, and high food prices are impacting millions more. Drought in Central America, and East and West Africa has deepened hunger across these regions and in Asia extreme storms inflict devastation in places like Vanuatu and the Philippines. At the same time, the Ebola epidemic in West Africa is fueling hunger by disrupting agriculture and other sectors, pushing millions already living on the edge deeper into poverty.

The U.N. Food and Agriculture Organization (FAO) estimates that today more than 800 million people go to bed hungry; one in five children is stunted—meaning their physical and cognitive development has been impaired by lack of proper nutrition; and every 7 seconds a child dies from hunger related causes.

INVESTING IN OUR GLOBAL PROSPERITY

There has been enduring bipartisan support for United States leadership in combating hunger not only because it is the right thing to do, but because that response is also part of our arsenal to advance the security and prosperity of the United States.

Fragile states, shrinking economies, and extreme poverty are not fertile ground for American businesses seeking foreign markets. And there is an emerging consensus that food insecurity joins with other factors to worsen instability in societies. Lack of access to food can trigger conflict and civil unrest as it did in more than 48 countries around the world during the food price crisis in 2008. Hunger can drive competition for water and land (food production resources) as we have seen in parts of Africa, and a vicious cycle can emerge of food insecurity driving conflict, which in turn further deepens food insecurity. Displacement and hunger driven by chronic poverty and recurrent crises can give incentives to individuals—including unemployed or underemployed youth—to join rebellions, criminal gangs, or extremist groups. Struggling families often take desperate measures as they seek to cope: men migrate in search of work, women may be vulnerable to trafficking or other forms of exploitation, girls are pulled out of school, children take to the streets to beg, and families begin to disintegrate.

Against the backdrop of a changing environment offering new options for aid delivery, a growing number of people affected by conflict and natural disasters, the rising costs of traditional food aid, and the tight budget environment the United States faces today—reforming U.S. food aid programs is a logical step to advance our economic and national security interests.

The President's FY16 proposal for reform, which requests a modest increase in our ability to provide food assistance not tied to procurement of United States food, would allow us to reach some 2 million additional people in food crises without an increase in budget. It also allows us to provide that assistance through means that promote growth and help the world's most vulnerable emerge from a cycle of extreme poverty and instability.

RATIONALE FOR FOOD AID REFORM

Gaining speed, saving money, improving recovery after emergencies

The Government Accountability Office (GAO) in a 2009 report found that purchasing food locally and regionally, rather than shipping it from the United States, is more cost-effective and greatly shortens delivery times.[1] For example, the study showed that buying food in Africa and Asia was 34 percent and 20 percent less expensive, respectively, than shipping food aid from the United States.[2] Studies by Dr. Chris Barrett of Cornell University show significant cost savings for many foods—such as bulk grains or pulses (lentils, peas, and beans)—ranging from 53 percent savings for the less expensive, local cereals to 25 percent for pulses.[3]

Response time is also generally faster and in an emergency, speed can mean the difference between life and death. The GAO found that food aid from the United States typically takes 4 to 6 months to reach beneficiaries while locally and regionally purchased food can reach those in need as much as 11–14 weeks sooner. The GAO found that shipping food from the United States to sub-Saharan Africa took 100 days longer than local or regional procurement. Moreover, having the option to use cash-based responses allows us to plan better because response times are shortened, particularly in cases where harvest conditions form the basis for needs.

It is true that the United States has improved in-kind food aid response times in recent years through prepositioning of food supplies. Today, at any one time, up to 60,000 tons of U.S. food stocks are in our prepositioning supply chain. This innovation has been invaluable. It does, however, add to overall costs and has certain constraints that limit its effectiveness. Limited shelf life for some commodities, repeated fumigations to keep commodities stored safely, uncertainty over what commodities will be needed where, and the appropriateness of an in-kind response, are all factors we must consider as we store food.

Speed and cost efficiency are not the only reasons we seek more flexibility. In some cases, giving a disaster survivor a food voucher or targeted cash transfer can reinforce economic recovery, support local farmers, generate jobs, reduce tensions, and create good-will toward the displaced for those hosting them and reinforce their appreciation for the American people and their generosity. At the same time, those receiving aid are accessing a more nutritious diet, including local fruits and vegetables, and have the dignity of choice to select items familiar to them and their families.

Ending monetization for sustainable development

I have been speaking almost exclusively about how food aid reform improves our emergency humanitarian responses. I would like to turn for a moment to our development efforts. USAID/Food for Peace administers 5-year development projects in many parts of the world to address the underlying causes of food insecurity. These programs are a vital part of USAID's agenda to build resilience in communities facing chronic poverty and recurrent crises, such as droughts and storms. For instance, in areas prone to drought, we train farmers to prevent soil erosion and conserve water so that they can increase their yields during dry periods. We teach mothers how to prepare healthy foods for their children and improve their access to nutritious foods to counter malnutrition. We facilitate better livestock management and help them diversify how they make a living, all so that they are better prepared to bounce back and are less reliant on humanitarian assistance when a crisis hits.

USAID/Food for Peace partners provide in-kind food to communities on the ground, while also carrying out development activities that address the underlying causes of food insecurity. Before the historic changes in the 2014 farm bill, we were limited under title II to fund these activities by buying food in the United States, shipping it overseas, and selling it so that we had local currency on hand to run the projects (i.e., monetization). According to a 2011 GAO study, USAID lost on average 24 cents on the dollar for monetization because on average it costs us more to buy and ship food than we can recover when we resell it abroad. According to the GAO this inefficiency meant that USAID "lost" $91 million through the monetization process over just the 3 year period analyzed.[4]

Having cash resources directly available means that USAID can simply provide partners with the resources they need to implement development activities, rather than burdening them with higher staff requirements and costs to implement the complicated and inefficient monetization process, freeing up time as well as valuable dollars that can be invested elsewhere. Last year, thanks in large part to the reforms in the farm bill, providing cash to partners rather than monetizing food aid allowed FFP to save $21 million and reached an additional 570,000 people.

FOOD AID REFORM PROGRESS TO DATE

Calls for food aid reform date back to the second Bush administration and it was ultimately the food price crisis of 2008, with millions of people suddenly unable to feed their families and civil unrest rapidly following the sudden price spikes, that led to Congress providing USAID with supplemental funds for food assistance interventions such as the local and regional purchase of commodities for the first time. In 2010, the administration requested and received funding for emergency food assistance in the base appropriation of the International Disaster Assistance (IDA) account, authorized through the Foreign Assistance Act. USAID used these funds to establish the Emergency Food Security Program (EFSP) to buy food locally and regionally and to provide targeted cash transfers or food vouchers so that people in food crises could buy food directly in local markets. At the same time, we put in place practices to ensure oversight and limit any potential for fraud or misuse of funds. This can range from the use of biometric identification practices to post-distribution monitoring that ensures food assistance is reaching the intended beneficiaries.

We prioritize these limited resources for programs where United States in-kind food aid cannot arrive in time or when other forms of food assistance are more appropriate, efficient, or cost-effective—such as in Syria. We did detailed analyses of a number of our 2012 EFSP programming and found results consistent with the GAO and Cornell University data on cost-savings, saving on average 33 percent by buying food locally and regionally compared to shipping similar commodities from the United States.

In the FY 2014 Budget request, President Obama proposed reforms to shift funding from title II into State/Foreign Operations foreign assistance accounts, mainly IDA and Development Assistance (DA). Under the proposal, up to 45 percent of IDA resources could be used for interventions such as local and regional purchases, cash transfers, and food vouchers. The USAID/FFP development programs would have been funded with Development Assistance funds, ending the need for monetization. We estimated that efficiencies gained from this proposal would have allowed us to reach an estimated 4 million additional people without an increase in funding for food aid.

While the proposed reforms were not adopted, USAID continued to press for reform through subsequent budget requests, as well as during the reauthorization of the farm bill. The 2014 farm bill advanced meaningful reform, offering USAID for the first time new flexibilities that increased the limited amount of cash available to support title II programs by seven percent to reduce monetization, purchase food locally and regionally, and help disaster victims access food in their local markets.

The administration's FY 2015 and FY 2016 title II budget proposals build on these past proposals and achievements and seeks an additional 25 percent of the $1.4 billion requested in title II funding for flexible food assistance programming. We estimate this will enable USAID to reach an additional 2 million emergency beneficiaries.

Why more flexibility is needed

The need for additional flexibility is clear. Despite these critical improvements to the title II program and the additional IDA resources that USAID/FFP has received over the past several years, much of the IDA has been needed has to meet the exponentially increasing needs in Syria. USAID/FFP now spends some $500 million a year to help meet the needs of more than 10 million Syrian displaced persons and refugees in the region. And let us be clear—without these flexible funds, we would not be able to feed people inside Syria and would have great difficulty feeding those displaced within the region, particularly where refugees are dispersed within host communities. Similar to our title II budget, our IDA budget for emergency food assistance for the rest of the world has remained stable since 2010, even as needs have grown in places like Sudan, the Central African Republic, northern Nigeria, and Ukraine. With regard to the new flexible funding in the farm bill, we have prioritized its use first and foremost to largely end monetization above the current statutory minimum required for the development programs.

With the cash flexibility we have, we still miss opportunities to run faster, more efficient, and effective emergency programs. Just this week we have learned that congestion in the port in Cameroon has disrupted the offloading of United States food, which in turn will delay its arrival in Chad, where refugees from the Central African Republic and Sudan are in need of emergency food assistance. And we have learned that increased global demand for United States sorghum will preclude our ability to buy this staple commodity for our programs over the next 4 months. Additional funds for local and regional procurement would not only help mitigate these kinds of unforeseen events, it would also allow us to help more of those in desperate need.

I want to emphasize that even as we seek additional flexibility, the majority of the title II request is for in-kind food. USAID will continue to need United States commodity food aid. Last year, for example, a large-scale in-kind food response was exactly the right response in South Sudan when conflict cut off millions and markets were not functioning. USAID provided nearly 120,000 metric tons to help save lives and pull South Sudan back from the brink of famine. With 3.5 million people projected to face extreme food insecurity by June, United States in-kind commodities will continue to be a critical part of USAID's response there. During the Sahelien drought of 2012 United States food arrived at the height of the lean season when markets were not well stocked; we provided just over 209,000 metric tons of United States food for that response. The President's FY 2016 proposal envisions continued need for United States in-kind food, both traditional commodities as well as United States manufactured specialized products to treat malnutrition, known as "blended" and "ready to use" foods. Many parts of the world do not manufacture these specialized nutrition products and they are playing an increasingly critical role in the prevention and treatment of malnutrition, especially for children.

HOW FOOD FOR PEACE USES EXISTING FLEXIBILITIES

I would like to share some examples of programs we have funded with the flexibility provided through the new farm bill and the IDA funding. From assisting refugees to responding to typhoons, food aid reform has allowed us to tailor our assistance to be more efficient, accountable, and responsive to local needs.

Syria

Since the onset of the Syrian crisis, USAID has provided more than $1.4 billion to respond to the needs of refugees as well as those impacted by conflict inside Syria. In the past, the Assad regime turned away United States food shipments, and regime and extremist attacks make it impossible to provide United States-branded food products. In response, our partners procure commodities regionally for pre-packaged food parcels for individuals and flour for bakeries to help feed more than

4.8 million people inside Syria. We are also supporting a debit card approach to provide food assistance to more than 2 million Syrian refugees in neighboring countries. Most Syrian refugees are not in camps but live in host communities widely dispersed geographically, many of them in towns and cities where markets are available. By providing a debit card with a prepaid sum, refugees can go to the market and choose a variety of foods, including fresh fruits and vegetables. The debit card not only drastically simplifies the distribution of food and provides greater choice, better nutrition, and dignity to Syrian refugees, but also eases the pressure on host countries by supporting their local economies. According to the U.N. World Food Programme (WFP), the food voucher program has created 1,300 new jobs and injected approximately $1 billion into the economies of Lebanon, Jordan, Turkey, Egypt, and Iraq since the program began. This also helps reduce the stress on host communities and build and sustain community support for refugees as the situation in Syria continues to deteriorate.

Last year, I had an opportunity to visit with a Syrian woman at a refugee camp in Turkey. She explained how the daily visit to the market helped to normalize what is not at all a normal situation. She fled her seaside town and a comfortable stone-built home where she lived with her two sons and their wives. Now she lives in a tent, sharing showers and other facilities with hundreds of others. The ability to shop on a daily basis and prepare foods familiar to her helps her get through the day.

Market-based approaches to reaching refugees and displaced people are increasingly preferred throughout the world and other major donors have modernized their food aid, adopting this approach. Current funding flexibilities would preclude the United States from shifting toward this approach for other refugee populations, including in Kenya and Ethiopia where these new methods are being brought to scale.

Philippines

In response to Super-Typhoon Haiyan in the Philippines in 2013 we used both United States in-kind food and cash-based assistance: we airlifted United States specialized foods that served as daily meal replacements for those who lost their homes, and we provided an immediate cash grant that allowed the U.N. and the Government of Philippines to tap into local rice stocks and distribute them within 5 days of the storm. Six weeks later, this help was supplemented by U.S. in-kind food—mostly rice—which arrived from prepositioned stocks in the region. And in the recovery phase, when markets had begun to function again, we supported a cash transfer program that allowed survivors to begin to access local markets again and revive local economic activity in the hardest hit areas. Had that storm happened at the end of the fiscal year when our limited pool of flexible funds was expended, our response would have been less timely, less effective, and more costly.

Kenya

In Kenya, we are using a variety of tools to build the resilience and address the emergency food assistance needs of the between 1 and 4 million Kenyans each year who do not have enough food during the lean season just before the harvest. In remote areas where people do not have easy access to markets, we provide in-kind food aid to meet needs. For those who can access markets in semiarid counties, we use electronic cash transfers for food purchases to avoid disrupting functioning markets and to support livelihoods. We are also providing farmers with the tools and know-how to increase their agricultural production, even during tough times.

Ndeli Samuel, a widow with four children, is training with other community members to learn new farming techniques that will save water when irrigating crops in the arid zones. In return, she receives a U.S. in-kind food ration for her participation because local markets are not accessible. Ndeli's training workshop was one of more than 700 resilience projects that USAID's implementing partner is undertaking to help farmers adopt simple but effective technologies to improve water and land use in the tough climate of Kenya's drylands. Ndeli says she is now ready to graduate and teach this technique to others in her community. She now grows enough crops for her family and is selling the rest to her neighbors. Here cash resources are critical so that we can help farmers buy better farming tools and train them in the farming techniques that helped Ndeli and her family increase their food security. These efforts are critical to USAID's resilience agenda, which seeks to help the world's most vulnerable build adaptive capacities so that they can mitigate and bounce back from droughts, conflict, and other risks they face.

CONCLUSION

Be it relief or development, USAID's food assistance programs are evolving based on years of experience, evidence-based learning and a willingness to innovate to assure hunger needs and United States interests are met in some of the world's toughest places. In our 60th anniversary year, we look back with pride at all that has been accomplished and look ahead, clear-eyed and focused, on the challenging work today's crises present to us. As part of USAID's mission to end extreme poverty and promote resilient, democratic societies, we are committed to continuing to find ways to work smarter and better so we can effectively and efficiently combat hunger around the globe. The President's food aid reform agenda furthers these goals.

I would be remiss if I did not close by saying that we in USAID/Food for Peace are proud to be entrusted with these resources and leading global humanitarian efforts to reach those most in need of food assistance. Our goal is to remain the best at what we do. We recognize our many partners who make this work possible and honor those who risk their lives or have lost their lives in their mission to deliver assistance to hungry people around the world.

We are proud to be carrying out this lifesaving work on behalf of the American people and appreciate the longstanding bipartisan congressional support for the mission of ending global hunger.

Thank you again for this opportunity to testify about why we have prioritized food aid reform as an agency and an administration. I look forward to your questions.

End Notes

[1] GAO, International Food Assistance: Local and Regional Procurement Can Enhance the Efficiency of United States Food Aid, But Challenges May Constraint is Implementation, June 2009.
[2] GAO, 2009, 16.
[3] Lentz, E., Barrett, C. B., & Gómez, M. I, "The Impacts of Local and Regional Procurement of U.S. Food Aid: Learning Alliance Synthesis Report."
[4] GAO, "International Food Assistance: Funding Development Projects Through the Purchase, Shipment, and Sale of U.S. Commodities Is Inefficient and Can Cause Adverse Market Impacts," June 2011.

The CHAIRMAN. Thank you. Thank you very much for what you and your staff do on behalf of our country. It is deeply appreciated.

Just to begin, what would be the implications for U.S. national security if you did not have the flexibility that you now have in Syria and in the region in delivering aid, and you had to rely solely on U.S. commodities?

Ms. ESPOSITO. Senator Corker, the Syrian example is a great one. I tried to describe in my testimony just how important it is to assuring that we are helping our allies address the tensions that can arise when so many people arrive in the country, stressing water services, social services. We have a very politically unstable situation, obviously. By providing this kind of assistance, we can help mitigate additional, further insecurity.

In Lebanon, for example, one in four persons is now a refugee. To put that in perspective, proportionally, that is like 80 million people coming to the United States in just a few years' time with little or no resources. So you can imagine the kind of tremendous stress that puts our allies under.

So this is part of our toolkit, part of our effort to mitigate instability within the region.

The CHAIRMAN. So, critics of us not purchasing food created in the United States say that it increases the chance of using unsafe food.

In the places where we have been able to use local and regional food, has this been a problem?

Ms. ESPOSITO. Senator Corker, I just want to underscore how seriously we take this issue. Whether we are using in-kind United

States food or locally procured food, food safety standards are rigorously followed.

Food safety standards of recipient countries must be met. We require testing for human pathogens and toxins. During the last 4 years, there have been no reports of unsafe food with regard to our local or regional procurement.

We are, though, remaining vigilant. We are expanding our commodity management training for all of our partners, and we have reissued our commodity management guide, which is relevant whether we are using in-kind food or locally and regionally procured food.

The CHAIRMAN. So if I hear you correctly, that allegation is a hoax.

Ms. ESPOSITO. We have no reports of unsafe food.

The CHAIRMAN. Okay.

Critics of reform also claim that cash-based programs transfer cash from the United States to corrupt governments, but we know that the aid is being provided directly to beneficiaries. So can you discuss this issue for us?

Ms. ESPOSITO. Thank you, Senator.

The in-kind food program, the voucher program, these programs are implemented by the same trusted partners who have been implementing in-kind food aid for the last 60 years.

You are right, we do not give any of our title II food assistance to governments. Our partners assess need independently. They target based on that need. They register people to be sure we can monitor who is getting the aid. We are relying on established financial institutions, including banks, to help with our transfers. And we have a series of new technologies that allow us to ensure that the resources are going to the people who need it the most.

So for example, the debit card program in Jordan and Turkey, we are able to track every item purchased in the grocery store because it is scanned with a barcode just like here, and we do not pay the vendors until we are sure that the funds were used properly.

So there are a lot of new ways, new tools, that we have available to us to mitigate the risk of unintended use for these resources.

The CHAIRMAN. So generally speaking, that criticism is a hoax. [Laughter.]

Ms. ESPOSITO. Whether in-kind or locally or regionally procured, we do all we can to ensure that there are no unintended uses of our resources.

The CHAIRMAN. I am sure there are examples, minor examples. But generally speaking, that is not the case.

Ms. ESPOSITO. That is correct.

The CHAIRMAN. So we are the only major developed country in the world that still provides the bulk of our food aid through domestic commodities.

Ms. ESPOSITO. Yes, Senator.

The CHAIRMAN. I think that kind of speaks for itself.

I just would like to know, does this make it more difficult for us to coordinate with other multilateral agencies and other donors in really hard-hit areas like Haiti, for example, in dealing with making sure that people have food when they need it?

Ms. ESPOSITO. Senator, the coordination really varies from country to country, and it depends on the context. So in some circumstances, there is certainly room for different approaches, depending on the nature of the problem.

I think the real challenge comes for our partners when other donors are requiring or asking for one modality, and we are, in turn, asking for different modality. So running dual types of platforms can be extremely complex for our partners. But it is very, very context specific.

The CHAIRMAN. So the other developed countries like us that care deeply about making sure that people have food, they have more flexibility. We are sort of locked in.

Ms. ESPOSITO. That is right. And they will press those partners to do the work in the most efficient way possible.

The CHAIRMAN. So as the perceived most innovative free nation in the world, we are really behind the rest of the world when it comes to feeding the poor. Is that correct?

Ms. ESPOSITO. Senator, we are a global leader in food assistance, and we are very proud of that leadership role. But we think that we could be more effective if we had additional flexibility.

The CHAIRMAN. Listen, thank you for being here, and I look forward to the questions from our distinguished ranking member.

Senator CARDIN. First of all, I join the chairman in thanking you for your incredible service to this country and to our global goals. It is a challenge because the world is never staying still and the challenges in the countries you are working in become very difficult at times, and you are still able to move forward. So we thank you very much for that.

Food aid cargo helps sustain U.S. commercially flagged fleets. There are concerns that if we change cargo preference, we may not be able to sustain the national defense sealift capabilities our military needs without significant additional Federal expenditures.

So how do you intend to balance the efficiency issues that you are trying to get in the food program with ensuring that we have adequate sealift capacity?

Did I stump you?

Ms. ESPOSITO. Could you repeat the question, please?

Senator CARDIN. Yes. Using U.S.-flagged vessels not only helps U.S. industry, but also helps the Department of Defense to have sealift capacity in the case of a national need. If you reduce the amount of food being shipped by U.S.-flagged vessels, it requires additional commitments by the Department of Defense to make sure that we have sealift capacity available in the case of emergency.

So how do you balance to make sure that the U.S. food program is contributing to our ability to be ready in the event of need by merchant marines?

Ms. ESPOSITO. Thank you, Senator, for clarifying the question.

The Department of Defense has released a statement supporting the President's fiscal year food aid reform proposal and its ability to improve our humanitarian responses. The Department of Defense stated that the proposal will actually not impact U.S. maritime readiness or its ability to crew surge fleet.

Senator CARDIN. That is not consistent with the information I have received, so I would appreciate if you could clarify that in specifics. I would be very interested to get a commitment from the Department of Defense that they would not be seeking additional resources to meet those needs.

If that is the case, I think we should have that on the record—that they can maintain their sealift capacity—because that is not consistent with other information that we have received.

Ms. ESPOSITO. Thank you, Senator. We can share the statement from the Department of Defense, but I, certainly, cannot speak on behalf of the Department of Defense.

Senator CARDIN. Let me go to my second point and that is that it is critically important that we are working with the international community. We cannot do this alone. But the U.S. Government cannot do it without our NGO partners. They provide a great deal of the help here. Yet, our NGO partners have concern about the legislation that is pending.

If we, on one hand, increase the government efficiencies but lose our private partners, the end result is less availability of food aid globally through the U.S. players.

So again, we still have concerns from the NGO community. How do you intend to resolve those issues?

Ms. ESPOSITO. Senator, we are open to dialogue with all the partners, be it maritime, our PVO partners to find the best way forward, so that we can find common ground and have a sustainable platform for this program moving forward.

With regard to flexibility, my perception is that there is actually great opportunity and have been new opportunities for PVO partners with the flexibility that we are garnering. We see an expansion of PVO responses in emergencies. They normally do not like to handle large commodity-based programs, but they have a lot of agility when it comes to these new types of approaches, local and regional procurement, electronic transfers.

So in Syria, for example, more than $100 million of our emergency money is going to PVOs to help with that response. In Haiti last year, we had both drought and hurricane and the entire emergency response was mounted on a PVO platform.

With regard to development, the flexibility we have garnered so far has eliminated the practice of monetization, which is this practice of buying food in the United States, shipping it overseas, and selling it.

I have heard just unanimous appreciation from that.

Senator CARDIN. There is no question there is reform here that they support. But, bottom line, there is still opposition because they believe it takes away their ability to fund their programs, that they need the flexibility. I think we have to work with the NGO community to resolve those issues.

I want to get to one other question, which is pretty fundamental. When I first came to the U.S. Congress in 1987, we could not pass a foreign aid bill. There are many reasons we could not do it, but there was a lack of support among the American people in understanding the role that we play in international development assistance as part of our national security budget. That was part of it.

But we did not advertise well that the fact that most of the foreign aid is American-produced products. And when that got better understood, we got more support. And we have strong support for this program because U.S. agriculture says, look, we are selling our products. We are selling them to the government. The government is then using it for international development assistance. So it is a win-win situation. And it acts, in many respects, as a counter-cyclical problem for American farmers. Now we are saying we are going to cut that back.

How do you intend to be able to maintain the strong support that we have in this country from the agricultural community when fewer American farm products are going to be used for development assistance?

Ms. ESPOSITO. Senator, thank you for that question. I think, as we all know, the agricultural products in the United States have been the backbone of the aid program for 60 years. We expect that they will continue to be key partners in future operations.

I mentioned the South Sudan program, and there are many others where we will continue to require American in-kind food aid.

But I would point out that because of rising food and fuel prices and the cost of doing business, there has actually already been a very significant decline in the amount of food that is used in the relief programs. So today we actually represent less than 1 percent of the total food that is shipped overseas.

And there is such a strong commercial demand right now. And we actually compete with those commercial demands when we buy our food. So for example, we heard even just last week that we are not going to be able to buy sorghum or we should not expect to buy sorghum in the United States over the next 4 months because global demand is so high that there is just a lack of availability of that.

So on the one hand, I would like to think that U.S. farmers will see that they will continue to play a vital role and that the American people will see that by doing this program more efficiently and more effectively, we continue to meet our national security and humanitarian interests.

Senator CARDIN. Thank you.

The CHAIRMAN. Thank you, Senator.

Senator Gardner.

Senator GARDNER. Thank you, Mr. Chairman.

And thank you to the director for being here this morning.

I am a little nervous. I see that Senator Coons has stepped out. I have been following him at every single meeting today so far. I do not know what I am missing, so I hope you will let me know, if his staff is here, if there something I should be at.

But I do want to thank the director for the opportunity to be here. I have a couple questions for you. I came in halfway through your testimony, so I want to maybe ask some things that you covered in that.

In your testimony, you state that while we are getting less for our dollar with the United States in-kind food assistance and the need for food assistance, it talks about we are getting less for our dollar with U.S. in-kind food assistance.

What do you mean by that statement? Are you talking about price? You are talking about commodity prices?

Ms. ESPOSITO. Thank you, Senator, for the question.

So as an example, in the early 2000s, it used to cost us $400 a ton to buy, ship, and program a ton of food overseas. Today, it is more than $1,200.

Senator GARDNER. The first number was?

Ms. ESPOSITO. $400.

Senator GARDNER. $400, now it is $1,200.

Ms. ESPOSITO. Correct.

Senator GARDNER. And what is a ton of food. You are not just referring to peas, lentils, beans? What you are referring to when you say a ton of food?

Ms. ESPOSITO. So it is an average cost, but it does include grains, peas, as you said, lentils, and vegetable oil are the primary basket that we ship.

Senator GARDNER. But usually no produce kinds of things?

Ms. ESPOSITO. Correct.

Senator GARDNER. Apples.

Ms. ESPOSITO. Correct.

Senator GARDNER. And that is because of the shipping and the long shipping times.

Ms. ESPOSITO. That is correct, Senator.

Senator GARDNER. Now will that change a little bit because you have some prices down? I think winter wheat is $4.97 a bushel in Byers, CO, today. Corn is down to its probably pre-2007 levels in some places. That changes up and down. It ebbs and flows.

Ms. ESPOSITO. That is correct.

Senator GARDNER. The study that you cite in your testimony by Dr. Barrett at Cornell talks about buying food in Africa and Asia. It was 34 percent and 20 percent less expensive, respectively.

Did that study take into account perhaps farm programs within those countries that may or may not provide certain subsidies to their farmers that they do not here, just out of curiosity?

Ms. ESPOSITO. I do not have the specific countries, Senator. I do know that they are extremely poor countries in Africa. And to my knowledge, there are not farm subsidy programs in those countries.

Senator GARDNER. Okay, so you are not talking about buying it for us to use there. We are talking about helping them build a sustainable base of agriculture. That is what you are talking about.

Ms. ESPOSITO. That is correct.

Senator GARDNER. Okay. I wanted to make sure that is what it was talking about and not simply saying that we are buying it to subsidize.

Let us say lentils, what percentage of U.S. production does U.S. food aid represent for the in-kind side of Food for Peace?

Ms. ESPOSITO. Senator, thank you for the question.

I am not sure about lentils per se, but altogether, it is less than 1 percent of our——

Senator GARDNER. But it is not 50 percent. We are talking about a very small fraction of U.S. production. I would think that an economist would not argue that you are driving and setting the market price. I would not think that that is the case.

So giving you the flexibility that you need to provide more specific or a better form of aid, if that means displacing some kind of in-kind production, it would be better for you and better for our partners, correct?

Ms. ESPOSITO. Yes, Senator.

Senator GARDNER. Thank you.

And then I may have missed this in your testimony, is there a balance and does it change year by year between in-kind contributions of U.S. aid and cash assistance? How do you prepare for that? I mean, does it depend country by country, situation by situation?

Ms. ESPOSITO. Senator, it is very context-specific. So we discussed the Syria example where it would not be appropriate to use the in-kind food. On the other hand, in South Sudan, and in the Sahelian countries during drought, we use substantial sums of food.

So food aid reform does not mean necessarily it is always going to be exactly the same amount every year, the balance. But we do think it is going to give us the flexibility to get the right tool at the right time.

Senator GARDNER. It does mean flexibility. Yes, very good. Thank you.

Thank you, Mr. Chairman.

The CHAIRMAN. Thank you.

I know you were not feeling particularly well when you came in. I hope the response you got today makes you feel a little bit better. We, certainly, thank you for being here.

I do want to make a comment, which may generate the need for a response from others, but it is not USAID's job to ensure that our military policy and sealift capacity is met, is it?

Ms. ESPOSITO. No, sir.

The CHAIRMAN. That is sort of a DOD problem, is it not?

Ms. ESPOSITO. Yes, Senator.

The CHAIRMAN. I would just say, look, I realize we have some sensibilities that will have to be dealt with. I would hope that the reason Americans, whether they are in the agriculture business or the maritime business or whatever, or the NGO business, especially the NGO business, would support us making changes because other people will not starve.

I would hope that people would support this because it is an important American value. And I hope that as we move through this, in spite of the fact that, let us face it, people make a living off U.S. programs, in some cases to the adversity of people who are starving, I would hope we would figure out a way to first prioritize the great work that you are doing and this American value that exists for this program. So thank you.

I think there may be a response.

Senator CARDIN. Thank you, Mr. Chairman. You got my attention, you did.

I strongly support our food program and our development assistance programs. I always have. And I would like to see a larger share of the budget and have said that publicly and will continue to support that.

I also want to make sure that every dollar we spend is used in the most efficient way. So I agree with the chairman on that point.

We cannot justify inefficiencies in any of our programs. So I agree with you.

But I regret that many Americans do not share our view of the importance of development assistance and instead say that we have not taken care of problems at home. You have to do that first.

We do both, and we could do a better job at both. But our success in these programs depends upon broad support. And the issues that are being raised with the U.S.-flagged vessels, with the NGO community's partnerships, and dealing with the agricultural community, are sensitive issues that I know the chairman understands and ones I think we need to be sensitive to as we try to pass a reform bill.

That was my only reason for raising it, but I want to have more efficiencies in the programs. We have broad support for the reforms that are in your proposal by all sectors of the stakeholders.

And what I said originally, I think this is an area where we should be able to try to get together on.

The CHAIRMAN. And, as you mentioned, coming in, I am sure, that based on what has happened over the last week, we, certainly, should be able to deal with this.

I would say that one of the things that would hit a chord, I think with every American, is using even the same dollars that we are spending—the same dollars that we are spending—to reach millions more to make sure they are not starving. And with the passage of this legislation, we, certainly, could make that happen.

Senator GARDNER. Thank you, Mr. Chairman. I think it goes back to some of the questions I was asking.

In the House of Representatives, I represented a district that was the 11th most-agricultural district out of 435 districts. Colorado has some of the highest wheat- and corn-producing counties in the Nation. Growing up in an implement dealership, I never remember farmers coming in and saying, well, you know, USAID is doing this or that to the program, therefore, I think market prices are going to be dropping today, or we are really going to do well because of it. The talk was what we can continue to do to help our partners.

So I think flexibility is key, knowing that it is not about what price is, it is not about the affected market is going to do that day because of a program, because you are talking about 1 percent or less of a commodity, and maybe more in some cases, but you are not talking about a market-setting kind of rate. So that should not be a part of the conversation.

What ought to be a part of the conversation is giving the tools, the flexibility, and the resources we need to best provide our neighbors around the world with the aid they need so they can grow up with more opportunity instead of less.

The CHAIRMAN. Very good. Thank you.

Thank you. Goodbye. [Laughter.]

Okay, we will now turn to our witnesses on the second panel. Our first witness is Mr. David Ray, vice president for policy and advocacy at CARE USA. Mr. Ray has over 20 years of experience working at CARE USA. Founded in 1945, it is one of the largest and oldest humanitarian aid organizations focused on fighting global poverty.

CARE USA is an important implementing partner of the Food for Peace program and was an early adopter of some of the food aid programs we are discussing today.

I thank you for allowing my daughter to intern with you in Tanzania years ago. It had a huge impact on her life. I thank you.

Our second witness is Dr. Vincent Smith, professor of economics at the Montana State University and visiting scholar at the American Enterprise Institute. Dr. Smith's research includes an examination of agricultural science policy, domestic and world commodity markets, risk management, and agricultural trade policy. He has authored nine books and monographs, and published over 100 articles on agriculture and other policy and economic issues.

Our third witness is Dr. Stephanie Mercier, a senior policy adviser at the Farm Journal Foundation. Prior to that, Dr. Mercier—am I pronouncing it correctly?—was a chief economist at the Senate Agriculture Committee from 1997 to 2011. Thank you for your service here. She was involved in several reform efforts made to the Food for Peace program.

With that, I will recognize Dr. Ray.

Thank you all for being here. We look forward to your testimony and your assistance in helping us navigate these issues. Thank you.

STATEMENT OF DAVID RAY, VICE PRESIDENT FOR POLICY AND ADVOCACY, CARE USA, WASHINGTON, DC

Mr. RAY. Chairman Corker, Ranking Member Cardin, members of the committee, thank you for the invitation to testify here today. I am David Ray, vice president of CARE, a global humanitarian organization.

As you mentioned, Senator, CARE was founded in 1945, when 22 American organizations sent what became known as care packages to the starving survivors of World War II. CARE's work now stretches across 90 countries, reaching more than 72 million people in 2014.

CARE has been a partner of the Food for Peace program for the past 60 years. While we are proud to be part of this great effort, even good programs can be made better. CARE has been a longtime champion of reforming title II funding to make it more flexible, effective, and efficient.

In fact, we believe in food aid reform so strongly that we put it over our own pocketbook. In 2006, CARE voluntarily ended our participation in open market monetization, the practice of purchasing commodities here; shipping them to developing countries; and then selling them, often at a loss, in order to generate funds for development programs. This decision has cost CARE more than $45 million annually in Federal funding since that time.

While the proceeds of monetization can be put to good use, a GAO report estimated that monetization results in an average loss of more than $.30 on the dollar. Research has shown that open-market monetization also risks destabilizing local markets by flooding them with low-priced U.S. commodities.

In fact, it was this potential to undermine the very small-scale farmers and communities we serve that prompted CARE to transition away from open market monetization.

Since that time, CARE has called for an end to the legal requirement to monetize, and we continue to push to make U.S. food aid programs more flexible, efficient, and effective.

Experience has shown us that while sending U.S. food is sometimes the appropriate thing to do, there are often more effective responses to crises. The cost of buying U.S. commodities and shipping them on U.S.-flagged vessels has proven to be as much as 30 to 50 percent higher than purchasing food locally or regionally, and it can take as much as three times longer to get food to the people who need it most.

Our point is this: Regulations governing the food aid program, with few exceptions, tie organizations like CARE to using one tool—U.S. commodities. It is like telling a carpenter, here is your toolbox but you can only use your screwdriver. Practitioners need flexible funding to use the right tools for the right jobs, whether it is cash transfers, vouchers, local or regional purchase, and/or efficiently transported U.S. commodities.

For example, CARE is working in Haiti to establish a country-led food voucher programs targeting the poorest 10 percent of the population. CARE's program called Kore Lavi, which translates to "Support Life," provides eligible participants with vouchers to buy locally produced staple and fresh foods. It also distributes four to five U.S. commodities to supplement the diets of pregnant and lactating women and children under the age of 2 who are in the critical thousand days window.

The program does four main things. First, it allows the most vulnerable to access locally produced fresh and staple foods and badly needed nutritional support, and to do so with dignity. Second, it allows participants to save their scarce resources, $500,000 so far, with the top two savings expenditures being school and medical fees. Third, it builds up the overall economy by creating demand for local farmers' products. Fourth, it reinforces the Haitian financial system as vendors receive payments through their formal banking accounts or through partner microfinance institutions.

Accountability is insured by providing participants with hologram imprinted identification cards, complete with their thumbprint, picture, and a unique ID number. There is oversight on what foods are sold, and there are in-person reporting stations for persons to report concerns or complaints.

Finally, because Kore Lavi was designed and implemented in partnership with the Haitian Government, the program is setting the ground for a sustainable assistance program that can be country-led and country-run in the future.

While Kore Lavi uses a mix of vouchers and in-kind commodities, there are times when only vouchers or commodities are needed. But U.S. commodities are just one tool in our toolbox, a tool that is not always appropriate and should not continue to be the required method of response for title II emergency and nonemergency programs.

In conclusion, Mr. Chairman, Ranking Member, CARE recommends that Congress increase the amount of flexible funding provided within title II to improve the cost-effectiveness of programs, enabling them to reach more people, save more lives, all at no additional cost to the taxpayer.

I thank the committee for its time, and I look forward to answering your questions.

Thank you.

[The prepared statement of Mr. Ray follows:]

PREPARED STATEMENT OF DAVID RAY

Chairman Corker, Senator Cardin, members of the committee, thank you for the invitation to testify here today and for the opportunity to present CARE's perspectives and experiences on international food aid reform. My name is David Ray, and I serve as the Vice President for Policy and Advocacy at CARE USA, a humanitarian organization that fights poverty and its causes around the world.

CARE traces its roots back to 1945, when 22 American organizations combined forces to rush emergency food rations in the form of "CARE Packages" to the starving survivors of World War II in Europe. Since that time, CARE's work has evolved and now stretches across 90 countries, reaching more than 72 million people in 2014. Last year, CARE's humanitarian projects supported more than 2.6 million people's access to quality food and improved nutritional well-being in 37 countries prone to, or affected by, conflict and disasters.

Ensuring that our Nation's international food aid programs achieve success at reducing hunger around the world is a critical challenge for all of us, and CARE shares your commitment to combating hunger by providing effective and accountable programming wherever it is needed.

FOOD AID REFORM AND CARE'S STORY

CARE has been a proud partner of the Food for Peace program for 60 years—a program with the explicit goal of combating world hunger and malnutrition and their causes, and promoting broad-based, equitable and sustainable development. CARE's work, together with the U.S. Government and implementing partners, has helped to save countless lives, and protect and improve the health and well-being of millions of people living on the edge of disaster.

And while CARE is proud to be a part of this great effort, even great programs can be made better. This is why CARE recommends that Congress increase the amount of flexible funding available through Title II "Food for Peace" funding—so that food aid dollars can be more effective and reach more people.

CARE's mission is to provide lasting, equitable, and sustainable development, which is guided by the needs and participation of the communities we serve. It's these principles, along with our nearly 70 years of experience, which inform our advocacy on international food aid reform and our implementation of food aid programs.

In 2006, CARE made the decision to voluntarily be the first, and only, NGO to end the practice of open-market monetization—a decision that cost CARE at least $45 million in federal funding every year. For those who are unfamiliar, open-market monetization is the practice of purchasing commodities here in the United States, shipping those commodities overseas, and then selling them—often at a loss—in order to generate funds for development programs. While the work of the resulting programs can be helpful, it is an inefficient practice. A GAO report estimated that monetization results in an average loss of 30 cents on the dollar.

Beyond being far less efficient than the logical alternative of simply providing cash to fund food security programs, open-market monetization is fraught with risk including the destabilization of local markets by flooding them with low priced U.S. commodities. It was this potential to undermine the very small-scale farmers and populations that we are aiming to serve, along with the need to stretch every dollar, which prompted CARE to transition away from open-market monetization. As of 2009, CARE no longer participates in, or takes any proceeds from, open-market monetization. Currently, CARE confines its use of monetized food aid to state-sponsored a relief program in Bangladesh that has a guaranteed return rate and involves targeted distribution in conjunction with the host government.

But, beyond the practice of monetization, CARE's experience has shown that taxpayer dollars for emergency and nonemergency U.S. food aid have the potential to go even further and to be even more effective.

Simply put, decades of experience has shown us that sending U.S. food is sometimes the appropriate thing to do, and sometimes it is not. Shipping food from the United States to developing countries is slow, expensive, and sometimes unpredictable. The cost of using U.S. commodities has shown to be significantly higher, in many cases 30–50 percent higher than alternative untied food aid purchased locally or regionally, and it can take as much as three times longer to get food to the people who need it most. CARE has seen the evidence showing that when U.S. commodities suffer untimely deliveries or are poorly targeted, it can have unintended, and sometimes harmful, economic consequences.

Moreover, U.S. commodities are often simply not enough to effectively address acute and chronic hunger. Practitioners need flexibility in food aid funding so that they can use a variety of tools to provide appropriate emergency and nonemergency responses that contribute to recovery, enhanced resilience and long-term development. For CARE, its partners, and other food aid actors, flexibility means having the option to use the right tools—whether it is cash transfers, vouchers, local/regional purchase, and/or efficiently transported U.S. commodities.

Our point is this: regulations governing the food aid program, with few exceptions, tie organizations like CARE to using one tool: U.S. commodities. It's like telling a carpenter, here's your tool box but you can only use your screwdriver to build my house.

Decisions about whether to distribute vouchers, to local or regionally purchase food, or to use food secured in the United States should be based on three factors: (1) Local market conditions; (2) the local or regional availability of food in sufficient quantities; and (3) the quality of that local food to meet local needs. Where markets work well, and food is locally available, cash transfers or vouchers are generally the most efficient. When food is locally available but markets do not function well, direct distribution of local or regionally purchased food is likely to be the most appropriate option, and where food is not locally or regionally available in sufficient quantity and quality, shipping food may be called for. If malnutrition is a critical issue, and foods available on the local market are not adequate to meeting nutrition needs, foods may need to be imported. In other instances a mix of these responses may be required.

KORE LAVI: AN EXAMPLE OF FLEXIBILITY

Recently, incremental food aid reforms in the 2014 farm bill took a step in the right direction by providing some increased flexibility in title II funding. These reforms have been leveraged with the cash-based Community Development Fund and the Emergency Food Security Program—both of which are outside of the title II programming and funded through the State-Foreign Operations Appropriations bill. As a result of this leveraging, we are beginning to show what untied, flexible food aid funding can do.

Using flexible funding out of the Community Development Fund and leveraging U.S. commodities provided through title II nonemergency support, CARE has established a promising voucher program in Haiti that is building the capacity of the Haitian Government and local markets to help support the most vulnerable and chronically malnourished members of the community.

As you know, the levels of poverty and food insecurity in Haiti have been long-standing, and were only intensified by the devastating 2010 earthquake. Currently, 60 percent of the Haitian population lives on less than $1.25 a day.

CARE's program, called Kore Lavi (which translates to "Life Support"), is targeting the bottom 10 percent of the Haitian population living below that $1.25 a day poverty line. The program is providing them with a mix electronic vouchers to buy locally produced staple foods and paper vouchers for the weekly purchase of fresh foods. Kore Lavi—as with all of CARE's voucher or cash transfer programs—was designed and is being implemented with strict commitment to oversight, accountability, and country ownership. In addition, there is visible USAID branding throughout the program, so that participants know where this assistance came from.

One the most important points of effectiveness and account ability in project design comes with the practice of identifying who needs services the most and who can participate in the program. CARE, along with a consortium of partners, has worked with the Haitian Ministry of Social Affairs to set up, populate, update, and run a database system of eligible participants, who were identified through an on-the-ground census that was executed by CARE and its partners. Both the composition of the food that the vouchers can redeem, along with their overall value ($25 USD, which covers approximately 30 percent of monthly dietary needs) was also decided in conjunction with the Haitian Government and in consideration of local market capacities.

The identified eligible participants were then provided hologram-imprinted identification cards complete with their thumb print, picture, and a unique identification number. This card can be taken to a participating vendor, often located in remote areas, on a monthly basis in order to receive their choice of a mix of six locally produced staple foods (corn, rice, millet beans, wheat, lentils, oil). There are strict vendor-limitations to only sell locally produced staple foods in order to rebuild market demand and support local agricultural production. Staple food vendors use mobile phones to access the participant database to verify the recipient, and to report what locally produced staple foods were provided. Once the transaction is verified, the vendor can redeem their payment through their formal bank account—a practice which is also helping to build up the Haitian financial system.

A similar system is also used by participants for the purchase of fresh foods at local markets through the use of time-limited and color-coded paper vouchers can be used throughout the month. Small-scale vendors of fresh foods, who are often women, are identified as a Kore Lavi vendor with a wide-brimmed hat and a branded ID badge (the hat enables illiterate consumers to identify these vendors). Because these small-scale vendors often do not have mobile phones or bank accounts, CARE has partnered with local microfinance institutions to provide same day vendor payment for the used paper vouchers—thus allowing for these small-scale vendors to meet their own food needs. Since CARE believes that accountability should run both ways, there are in-person reporting stations at each market for participants and vendors to report complaints and have their questions answered.

In addition to the electronic and paper vouchers, a special focus has been put on identifying and reaching vulnerable pregnant and lactating women, and children under the age of 2 who are in the critical 1,000 days window. These women and children are also eligible to receive additional rations of fortified U.S. commodities to help ensure their nutritional needs are met while still enabling them to access local, fresh foods.

Kore Lavi is now in its second year, and so far the program has reached approximately 125,000 chronically hungry individuals and has partnered with 387 vendors. Some program participants have accumulated savings with the money they have not spent as a result of using the vouchers. As of now, this collective savings amounts to approximately $500,000 through 20-cent deposits, with the top two savings expenditures going to pay for school and medical fees. In short, Kore Lavi supports participants' food security, allows them to participate in a formal market, save their scarce resources, and exercise their sense of dignity by being able to make their own food choices. In turn, local farmers are able to receive a fair price for their products, participate in a stronger market, and meet the needs of their community.

It is important to note that the participant database developed by Kore Lavi is in the process of being transitioned over to the Haitian Government, so that capacity is fully developed to maintain and update the database in the future. The end goal of the program is to transition the whole process over the Haitian Government. Because Kore Lavi was designed and is being implemented in conjunction with the Haitian Government, the program is laying the groundwork for a sustainable country-led assistance program that can be county-run in the future.

This is the type of work than can be done with funding flexibility food aid funding—work that not only addresses immediate needs, but builds a brighter future.

And, this is the kind of flexibility that CARE would like to see baked into title II funding, instead of having to patch together small-scale solutions due to the constraints of tied aid.

CONCLUSION

Kore Lavi is just one example of the type of programming that could be scaled up, replicated, or expanded with untied, flexible food aid funding. By taking advantage of the small amount of flexible funding currently available, Kore Lavi does not rely on monetization, therefore allowing CARE to support local businesses and ensure that taxpayer dollars are stretched as far as possible.[1]

While Kore Lavi uses a mix of vouchers and in-kind commodities, there are circumstances when a voucher-only approach is appropriate, and there are times when U.S. commodities are needed. In instances like South Sudan, where markets are broken and local/regional food is not available, in-kind food aid is valuable when it arrives on time and reaches the people who need it most. This is also the case for programs like Kore Lavi, where locally produced fortified foods are not available but badly needed for pregnant and lactating women. But, U.S. commodities are just one type of blunt instrument—an instrument that is not always appropriate and should not continue to be the required method of response for title II emergency and non-emergency programs.

In conclusion, although current law provides authority for limited cash assistance, CARE recommends that Congress increase the amount of flexible cash assistance provided within title II programs and consider new strategies on how best to make those resources available. Not only would this substantially improve the cost-effectiveness of both emergency and nonemergency programs, it would also result in more people being reached, more lives being saved, and more sustainable solutions to hunger and poverty.

Mr. Chairman, members of the ommittee, I thank you for your time and I look forward to answering your questions.

End Notes

[1] The Haitian Government specifically requested no monetization for this program. This request was consistent with findings of a Bellmon Analysis study, which also indicated that food aid monetization would be very problematic within the local economy. Therefore, CARE would have been unable to implement programs to address food security without use of limited flexible funding that is leveraged outside of title II, through the Community Development Fund.

The CHAIRMAN. Thank you very much.

Dr. Smith.

STATEMENT OF VINCENT SMITH, AEI VISITING SCHOLAR, PROFESSOR OF ECONOMICS, DEPARTMENT OF AGRICULTURAL ECONOMICS AND ECONOMICS, MONTANA STATE UNIVERSITY, BOZEMAN, MT

Dr. SMITH. Chairman Corker, Ranking Member Cardin, members of the committee, thank you so much for inviting me to speak with you today on this important issue.

From their inception, U.S. emergency and other food aid programs have accomplished a great deal in alleviating hunger, malnutrition, morbidity and mortality among the world's most desperately poor people. However, they simply have not been nearly as efficient and effective as they can be and should have been in providing the aid that mitigates the adverse effects of hunger and malnutrition among millions of children and adults.

A wide range of academic analyses that have already been cited and government reports are remarkably consistent in drawing the following conclusions about the current U.S. food aid program.

First, the current practice of using monetization to fund NGO programs is highly wasteful and inefficient, yielding less than $.70 of usable funds for every tax dollar expended. Many NGOs deserve to have their food and food-security-related programs funded, but the programs should be funded directly and efficiently with appropriate oversight about how the funds are used, to ensure they are effective and efficient programs.

Second, agricultural cargo preference is an exceptionally financially costly way of shipping food from the United States to the ports of entry in the regions where the aid is needed. A conservative estimate is that it increases the cost of shipping food on average under food aid programs by 46 percent, about $150 million a year in 2006 dollars, never mind current dollars.

As a result, the U.S. Government spends more on shipping food than on purchasing the food delivered, according to the GAO. In comparison, Canada in 2012, for example, used 70 percent of its food aid funds for food and only 30 percent for administration and transportation. Canada uses local sourcing, for example, and does not, to my knowledge, involve monetization.

Further, in combination with the current requirement that food aid be mainly sourced from the United States, the cargo preference requirement significantly contributes to otherwise unnecessary delays up to 2 months, as the chairman noted, in delivering emergency food aid. The impacts of these delays themselves have severe adverse effects, particularly on the morbidity status of children and their long-run ability to be productive citizens.

Agriculture cargo preference have been justified by private maritime interests as providing essential support and maintenance for a U.S. maritime fleet that can provide military prepared support vessels in time of war. The overwhelming weight of the empirical evidence, not just from DOD but from other studies, is that cargo preference as applied to food aid makes very little effective contribution to maintaining the military preparedness of the U.S. maritime fleet through providing additional mercantile fleet capacity that can be used by the Department of Defense.

Current estimates indicate that fewer than 11 relatively small ships and less than 500 sailors are affected by the foreign aid program. Those numbers are estimates and subject to question by everybody, but they are ballpark pretty accurate.

Maritime interests have also made a related claim that food-aid-related cargo preference creates many thousands of high-paying jobs that has a large effect on the U.S. economy, both by expanding the U.S. Merchant Marine Service and decreasing port service activities. Adding 500 jobs is not having a big impact on the economy, with apologies to everybody. And parenthetically, the funds being used for those jobs are being diverted from other activities that would generate economic activity, too.

The net effect of these programs on the economy is close to zero. I would be tempted to say negative, but then I would be a bigoted economist and I cannot say that.

A related important humanitarian concern is the food carried mainly under cargo preferences is mainly carried by old and slow ships, and that is probably contributing to the delay in delivering food from the United States.

The clear primary beneficiaries of cargo preference are the private maritime interests that largely support that program, particularly the companies that own the vessels. Many of these vessels would have been decommissioned as noncompetitive, both in intracoastal transportation and international transportation, were it not for the food aid program, at least that is the evidence that appears to come from the George Mason study that was referred to earlier and by the work by Bageant, Barrett, and Lentz.

Finally, I would like briefly to discuss the issues associated with local and regional sourcing of food aid. Permitting complete flexibility or as much flexibility as possible for USAID and other government food programs to locally and regionally source emergency aid and other forms of food aid is clearly a much more cost-effective way and faster method of delivering the needed aid than requiring sourcing from the United States.

That is not to say that no food will be sourced from the United States. Processed food is clearly optimally sourced right now from the United States in many contexts, particularly, for example, in relation to peanut butter and products like that.

The humanitarian impacts of allowing substantial flexibility in sourcing food, as has already been discussed in this session, are very substantial. A minimum estimate of 2 to 4 million people, and a maximum estimate of 8 million to 10 million people, would benefit by reallocating the funds to more flexible sourcing.

At the same time, permitting local sourcing will have no measurable economic impacts on income of U.S. farmers or the overall performance of the agriculture sector. In fact, if anything, having more money to buy food aid food in the form of wheat and corn, which wheat and corn is a global market, actually would enhance global demand for those foods. That would actually be of more benefit—although a minuscule benefit, it must be said—to the corn growers of Iowa and the wheat growers of Colorado and Montana.

In summary, ending these practices would generate tremendous benefits in terms of improving humanitarian aid, and they would benefit the United States in many domains—economically, politically, and in terms of the good will that we would accumulate around the world that is so important to all of our efforts to sustain a democratic and productive society.

Thank you, sir.

[The prepared statement of Dr. Smith follows:]

PREPARED STATEMENT OF DR. VINCENT H. SMITH

Chairman Corker, Ranking Member Cardin, and distinguished members of the committee, thank you for the opportunity to testify today about the future of U.S. food aid programs. I am honored to be invited to discuss these programs, their importance, and the need to reform them.

SUMMARY

The central goal of any government program should be to meet the program's core objectives as efficiently and effectively as possible. From their inception, U.S. Emergency and other Food Aid Programs have accomplished a great deal in alleviating hunger, malnutrition, morbidity, and mortality among the world's most desperately poor populations. However, they have not been nearly as efficient and effective as they can be and should have been in providing aid that mitigates the adverse effects of hunger and malnutrition of children and adults.

This has especially been, and continues to be, the case with respect to emergency food aid. A plethora of academic analyses and government reports (including a long sequence of General Accountability Office reports) have been remarkably consistent in drawing the following conclusions about the current U.S. food aid program.

1. The current practice of monetization (allowing NGOs to sell food aid food shipped from the U.S. in local markets and use the proceeds to fund their aid-related programs) is highly wasteful and inefficient. Many NGOs deserve to have their food aid and food security related programs funded, but the programs should be funded directly with appropriate oversight about how the funds are used to ensure they are effective and efficient.

2. Agricultural Cargo Preference (ACP) is an exceptionally financially costly way of shipping food aid from the United States to the ports of entry in the regions where the aid is needed. Worse, in combination with the current requirement that food aid be mainly sourced from the U.S., the cargo preference requirement significantly contributes to otherwise unnecessary delays in delivering emergency food aid. The impacts of these delays have themselves had severe adverse effects on, especially, morbidity and mortality rates among children.

3. Agricultural Cargo Preference has been justified by Maritime interests as providing essential support for the maintenance of a U.S. maritime fleet (including both ships and sailors) that will be essential for providing military preparedness needed to support the effective defense of the country in time of war.

The overwhelming weight of the empirical evidence is that ACP makes no, or at best minimal, effective contribution to maintaining the military preparedness of the United States through providing additional relevant and useable mercantile fleet capacity (in terms of both sailors and ships) for DOD purposes. In other words, the evidence makes nonsense of the claim that ACP plays any critical role with respect to U.S. military preparedness.

4. Maritime interests have also made a related claim that ACP creates many thousands of high paying jobs and has large effects on the U.S. economy, both by

expanding the U.S. merchant marine service and increasing port service activities as well as through what are called "multiplier effects."

A recent U.S. Department of Defense estimate of the direct marine service effects is that ACP increases the employment of sailors in the U.S. mercantile marine fleet by between 375 and 495 jobs a year. Those jobs cost the taxpayer an estimated annual average additional outlay about $100,000 per job over an above what would be otherwise be spent to transport U.S. food aid from the United States to the destinations where the food is needed. These are funds that annually, under the current food aid programs, are directly reallocated from providing food aid to over 2 million very poor people a year.

A related further important humanitarian concern is that food carried under cargo preference by U.S.-flag ships is typically carried on old and slow ships (which adds to the labor and other costs incurred through the cargo preference program), delaying the delivery of the emergency food aid to the children and adults who need it. Barrett and Lentz (2014) point out that such delays result in increased malnutrition and morbidity among, perhaps especially, children.

Almost no "multiplier effects" or broader economy-wide impacts derive from these maritime jobs, in part because they simply involve the reallocation of government funds from one use to another use, and in part because some of the international maritime sailor's income is inevitably directly spent in foreign economies. In addition, in any case, multiplier impacts associated with new government spending are relatively small (multipliers are almost never estimated to be larger than about 1.8).

5. The primary beneficiaries of the agricultural cargo preference mandate are the private shipping companies, whose vessels are approved for and used to carry food aid shipments under the ACP. Effectively, ACP is a straightforward and relatively wasteful form of corporate welfare that imposes substantial humanitarian costs on some of the poorest and most desperately in-need families and children in the world by reducing the effectiveness of U.S. Food Aid programs.

6. Permitting complete flexibility, or as much flexibility as possible, for USAID and other government food aid programs to locally and regionally source emergency and other forms of food aid is a more cost-effective and faster method of delivering the needed aid than requiring sourcing from the United States. The humanitarian impacts of allowing substantial flexibility in souring food aid have consistently been estimated be very substantial, reducing nutrition deficiency related morbidity and mortality for an average of over 4 million children and adults on an annual average basis.

At the same time, permitting local and regional sourcing will have no measurable economic impacts on the incomes of U.S. farmers or the overall performance of the U.S. agricultural sector. Paradoxically, for many of the crops raised by U.S. producers and used as food aid—such as corn, wheat, and rice—if anything a shift to local and regional sourcing will have positive, rather than negative, effects on the prices they receive for their crops. The reason: these are crops traded in global markets and a more efficient use of U.S. food aid funds will increase global use and demand for those crops, albeit in very modest amounts relative to the global production of wheat, corn, rice, and other food aid commodities.

AGRICULTURAL CARGO PREFERENCE: ISSUES AND EVIDENCE

The following issues are central to any assessment of agricultural cargo preference as the policy is applied to U.S. emergency and other food aid:

(a). Does the U.S. cargo preference program as applied to U.S. food aid programs have a substantial and adverse impact on the cost of delivering food aid to the people who desperately need that aid?

(b). Does the food aid related U.S. agricultural cargo preference program in any substantive way enhance the military preparedness of the United States by expanding the capacity of the private U.S. merchant marine service to support U.S. military efforts in other countries?

(c). Who are the primary beneficiaries of the government revenues that have to be spent as a result of the food aid related U.S. cargo preference program? Is this just corporate welfare in disguise?

(d). Does the food aid related U.S. cargo preference program have substantive positive impacts on the U.S. economy either through job creation within the U.S. mercantile marine or by creating additional economic activity?

(a). Does the U.S. cargo preference program as applied to U.S. food aid programs have a substantial and adverse impact on the cost of delivering food aid to the people who desperately need that aid?

The evidence on the impact of cargo preference on the delivery costs of U.S. food is unambiguous and large and is derived from multiple analyses by different sources. Perhaps the most careful academic study to date, by Bageant, Barrett and Lentz (2010), using conservative assumptions about the nature of the U.S. Department of Transportation Marine Administration data available on food aid shipping costs, estimates that food shipped on U.S.-flagged cargo preference vessels costs 46 percent more than shipping the same aid at competitive rates. A more recent independent study by a research group at George Mason University obtained very similar estimates.

Quite stunningly, in fiscal year 2012 (October 1, 2011 to September 30, 2012) the General Accountability Office (2014) reported that 45 percent of Food for Peace funds was spent on food aid transportation while only 40 percent of those funds was spent on food aid. In contrast, for example, Canada spends 70 percent of its food aid budget on food aid (Barrett and Lenz, 2014). While part of the reason for the exceptional proportion of total U.S. Food for Peace program outlays allocated to transportation is the current mandate to source most food aid from the U.S. rather than from local or regional markets closer to the areas of need, the impact of the cargo preference requirement on those costs, conservatively estimated to be about $150 million a year, is also substantial.

(b). Does the food aid related U.S. agricultural cargo preference program in any substantive way enhance the military preparedness of the United States by expanding the capacity of the private U.S. merchant marine service to support U.S. military efforts in other countries?

The empirical evidence is also surprisingly clear on this issue. Cargo preference for food aid does little or nothing to increase the ability of the private companies that form the U.S. Maritime Service to provide services to the Department of Defense (DOD) in time of a major war. That is, applying cargo preference requirements to food aid shipments has no effective impact on the military preparedness of the United States. Two relatively recent detailed analysis of registration (Bageant, Barrett and Lentz, 2010; George Mason University, 2015) have concluded that the overwhelming majority of U.S.-flagged ships approved for transporting foreign aid under the cargo preference mandate do not meet the criteria established by the Department of Defense for a mercantile ship to be viable for military purposes (only 17 of 61 ships appeared to meet the DOD criteria in 2006). Tellingly, most of the ships fail on to meet the DOD criteria on two important grounds: they are too old and they cannot be readily used as roll-on/roll-off or liner container ships (they are bulk carriers or tankers) (Button, et al, 2015). Employment effects associated with the food aid cargo preference mandate are also very modest.

The program is estimated by the Department of Defense to increase employment in the mercantile marine by between about 350 and 495 sailors with U.S. citizenship. In terms of the potential contribution of these individuals to the military preparedness of the United States, when compared to the numbers of navy personnel who leave the U.S. Navy and Coastguard each year (well in excess of 30,000), many of whom can be rapidly retrained to serve as mercantile marine support personnel, these numbers are very modest. The estimated additional cost to the Federal Government of hiring these additional 350–495 sailors is approximately $100,000 per sailor (Bageant, et al, 2010; Button, et al, 2014).

Additional so-called ''multiplier effects'' almost certainly do not exist for two reasons. First, allocating the funds in other ways would have similar initial employment effects in term of numbers of jobs for U.S. citizens (though not in the mercantile marine service) and, second, multiplier effects are, in fact, much smaller than indicated some recent mercantile marine industry supported studies, recently reviewed by Button, et al (2015), have claimed. In the context of an economy that is enjoying some growth, a multiplier effect of one may be too small, but a multiplier effect of two is almost surely much too large, and one of 8.6 (a number used in one study of the employment effects of agricultural cargo preference program) is simply the product of a lively imagination.

(c). Who are the primary beneficiaries of the government revenues that have to be spent as a result of the food aid related U.S. cargo preference program? Is this just corporate welfare in disguise?

The older U.S.-flag ships typically used for carrying cargo preference food aid have been estimated to have much higher operating costs than U.S.-flag ships used to transport goods between U.S. ports because, as they have aged and become slower, these ships become much more expensive to run in terms energy efficiency, labor requirements, and other costs associated with maintaining them (Button, et al; Bageant, et al). These additional costs associated with the U.S.-flagged older ships mean that they would almost surely not be competitive with other carriers in almost any other market (including ocean-based transshipment between U.S. ports that requires cargo preference carriage by U.S.-flag ships).

Thus, one reasonable interpretation of the food aid cargo preference program is that it allows the companies who own those ships to continue to make profits from them (Bageant, et al; Barrett and Lentz; Button, et al.). Effectively, therefore, the primary beneficiaries of the food aid cargo preference program are the companies that own the U.S.-flag ships that carry those cargos. Some of the U.S. registered shipping companies, several of which appear to be owned and controlled through holding companies by large foreign-based multinationals, seem to exist primarily because that is the way through which those companies can access economic profits from the food aid cargo preference program. Without that program, those older ships, which apparently do not meet the DOD criteria for militarily useful vessels, would otherwise be decommissioned.

(d). Does the food aid related U.S. cargo preference program have substantive positive impacts on the U.S. economy either through job creation within the U.S. mercantile marine or by creating additional economic activity?

Any employment effects are trivial and, in fact, it is not clear that they are positive. Allocating the approximately $100,000 per mercantile marine job elsewhere in the U.S. economy could well have larger employment effects, depending on where the funds were allocated. The central public policy issue has nothing to do with employment per se, but with whether the food aid component of the cargo preference program increases military readiness in any substantive way. The answer provided by independent assessments of the program is consistently that such is not the case.

LOCAL AND REGIONAL SOURCING: ISSUES AND EVIDENCE

The evidence is unambiguous. As Lentz and Barrett (2014) and previous studies have consistently reported (for example, GAO, 2009; Barrett and Maxwell, 2005) local and regional sourcing result in substantial cost savings. Equally importantly, economically efficient sourcing from optimal suppliers and locations substantially reduces the time taken to deliver emergency food aid to where it is needed, dramatically reducing the morbidity and mortality effects on the target populations (Lentz and Barrett).

A politically relevant question is whether allowing for complete flexibility in sourcing food aid would adversely affect U.S. farmers. Most food aid involves commodities traded on global markets such as corn and wheat. To the extent that food aid reform, crucially including a shift to local and regional sourcing, will enable the U.S. Government annually to purchase 50 to 60 percent more food aid with any given food aid budget (Lentz and Barrett), the impact will be to increase global annual demand for crops such as corn and wheat.

Clearly, the net effect would therefore be to increase average prices received by U.S. and other farmers for those commodities. It is important to emphasize, however, that for commodities like corn, wheat, and rice, U.S. food aid makes up very small proportions of total world consumption and therefore any price effects would essentially be unobservable. Even for small acreage commodities like peas and lentils, impacts on prices received by U.S. farmers as a result of food aid purchases appear to be very small. For processed commodities like peanut butter, it currently appears that the U.S. remains the optimal source for obtaining food aid. Hence economic impacts on U.S. agriculture from ending the U.S. sourcing mandate are likely to be very small and, in terms of prices received by U.S. farmers could be beneficial (although miniscule in size).

THE PRACTICE OF MONETIZATION

Monetization, the practice of shipping U.S. food to foreign destinations to be sold by nongovernment agencies in commercial markets to obtain cash to be used for other aid related projects, is simply a waste of resources (see, for example, GAO, 2011; Lentz and Barrett, 2014). The practice results in the NGOs obtaining 70 to 75 cents for every dollar of tax funds used in the monetization process. A much more effective use of such funds would be simply to provide the NGOs with grants to accomplish the relevant aid related objectives. Unequivocally, to ensure that such funds are used for the intended purposes, USAID and USDA would have to carefully monitor their use, but such monitoring is already needed in the context of the monetization process.

References

Bageant, E.R., C.B. Barrett and E. C. Lentz. "Food Aid and Cargo Preference." Applied Economic Perspectives and Policy, 4, 2010, 624–641.

Barrett, C., and E C. Lentz. "Highway Robbery on the High Seas." The Hill, May 30, 2014.

Barrett, C.B., and D.G. Maxwell. "Food Aid After Fifty Years: Recasting Its Role." London, Routledge, 2005.

Button, K., W. Ferris, and P. Thomas. "The Political Economy of Shipping Food Aid Under the Cargo Preference Regime." School of Public Policy, George Mason University, MS–3B1, 2015.

George Mason University. "Impact of Government Food Aid Reforms on the U.S. Shipping Industry: Preliminary Results." 2015.

Lentz, E.C., and C.B. Barrett. "The Negligible Welfare Effects of the International Food Aid Provisions in the 2014 Farm Bill." Choices, 3rd Quarter, 2014.

U.S. AID. "Food Aid Reform: Behind the Numbers." Fact Sheet, 2013.

U.S. Government Accountability Office. "International Food Assistance: Local and Regional Procurement Can Enhance the Efficiency of U.S. Food Aid but Challenges May Constrain Its Implementation." 2009. GAO–09–570.

U.S. Government Accountability Office. "International Food Assistance: Funding Development Projects Through the Purchase, Shipment and Sale of U.S. Commodities is Inefficient and Can Cause Adverse Market Impacts." 2011, GAO–11–636, Washington DC.

U.S. Government Accountability Office. "International Food Aid Prepositions Speeds Delivery of Emergency Food Aid But Additional Monitoring of Time Frames and Costs is Needed." 2014, GAO–14–277, Washington DC.

The CHAIRMAN. Thank you, Doctor.
Dr. Mercier.

STATEMENT OF STEPHANIE MERCIER, SENIOR POLICY AND ADVOCACY ADVISER, FARM JOURNAL FOUNDATION, ALEXANDRIA, VA

Dr. MERCIER. Mr. Chairman, Ranking Member Cardin, members of the committee, thank you for holding this hearing today on the critical topic of U.S. international food aid. I appreciate the opportunity to provide testimony on this matter.

I am Stephanie Mercier and I serve as the senior policy and advocacy adviser for the Farm Journal Foundation. The foundation has not taken a formal position on this issue, so this testimony reflects my views alone. I also would like to note that I worked as a consultant for a number of humanitarian NGOs over the last few years as well.

I worked on food aid policy issues for about the last 18 years, primarily as part of my portfolio on the Democratic staff of the Senate Agriculture Committee between 1997 and 2011. In that role, I helped to lead the committee's work on the trade title in two farm bills, in 2002 and 2008, and we were able to make modest reforms in the direction of improved efficiency and flexibility for the title II program in both bills.

Those modest reforms were continued in the 2014 farm bill passed in February of last year. The reforms to the Food for Peace program proposed in the bill introduced by the chairman and Senator Coons in February would take a giant stride further down that path.

In the 2002 farm bill, Congress first began to recognize that the traditional mode of U.S. assistance did not always offer the optimal response. This approach consists of purchasing and shipping U.S.-sourced commodities after a natural disaster or conflict had already occurred and people were already going hungry. In that bill, Congress authorized USAID to set up prepositioning warehouses that allowed them to hold commodities that could be quickly dispatched when emergencies arose.

Congress expanded the authority for prepositioning in the 2008 farm bill, allowing USAID to establish additional sites. The bill also increased its share of title II funding that could be used to cover certain types of nonfood expenses from around 5 percent previously to a maximum of 13 percent.

The other major milestone in the 2008 farm bill was the establishment of a pilot program to test whether or not efficiency gains might be available from allowing U.S. resources to be used to purchase food locally or regionally, rather than insist on always being U.S.-sourced commodities.

Independent studies of that LRP pilot found that buying locally was less expensive for most commodities and that the food on average delivered in about half the time as it took for food that was sourced and shipped from the United States.

The 2014 farm bill moved that dial on reform further. It raised the share of title II funds that could be used to cover nonfood expenses from 13 to 20 percent, and expanded the category of eligible expenses. That legislation also authorized the standing LRP program for up to $80 million dollars annually to be run by USDA in part as a complement to the school feeding program that they operate.

To augment the limited flexibility available under current Food for Peace rules, USAID established the Emergency Food Security Program, or EFSP, in 2010. It was designed to utilize LRP and other cash-based mechanisms under the broad authority of the Foreign Assistance Act, giving them some ability to tailor the U.S. response to the variety of circumstances under which international food assistance is needed.

There has been a lot of reference to Syria already in this hearing. I think that is a perfect example of how flexibility can be used to great advantage.

I would like to point out, however, that there is no need to assume that the legislation that Senators Corker and Coons introduced would necessarily turn title II into an entirely cash-based program. We know from the results of the pilot program that there are some commodities—vegetable oil, in particular—that are actually cheaper to produce and ship from the United States than they are to buy locally through recipient countries.

We also know that there will always be some situations where the problem is simply that there is not enough food in the local area. For those beneficiaries, sourcing U.S. food and shipping it is still going to be the best solution.

In its early years, the Food for Peace program was an important component of U.S. agriculture policy. In 1957, in fact, it was estimated that U.S. food had accounted for about 30 percent of all U.S. ag exports. Today, however, food aid shipments account for less than 1 percent of total ag exports.

While U.S. farmers continue to take justifiable pride in providing food for hungry people, this program is no longer really viewed by most in agriculture as a key engine of economic growth for their industry.

For the last several decades, the United States has been the leading provider of humanitarian food assistance around the world, and that is a status we must maintain. However, that assistance is still delivered primarily by a mechanism that was appropriate for the market environment of the 1950s but no longer adequately meets the needs of the people the program is intended to serve.

It is past time for U.S. food aid to enter the 21st century. Congress should allow USAID to provide the type of assistance that can be tailored to the complex environment where hungry people around the world are often found.

Thank you for the opportunity to testify, and I am ready to answer any questions you might have.

[The prepared statement of Dr. Mercier follows:]

PREPARED STATEMENT OF DR. STEPHANIE MERCIER

Mr. Chairman, Ranking Member Cardin, members of the committee, thank you for holding this hearing today on the critical topic of international food assistance that the United States provides to hungry people around the world. I appreciate the opportunity to provide testimony on this matter.

I am Stephanie Mercier, the Senior Policy and Advocacy Adviser for the Farm Journal Foundation. The Foundation has not taken a formal position on the issue of food aid reform, so any opinions expressed in my testimony are mine alone. In the last 3 years, I have also served as a consultant to a number of humanitarian NGOs who support reform of U.S. food aid programs. That group includes CARE, which is represented on this panel by Mr. David Ray, their Vice President for Policy and Advocacy, as well American Jewish World Service, Bread for the World, and Oxfam America, among others.

I have worked on food aid policy issues for about 18 years, primarily as part of my portfolio as chief economist for the Democratic staff of the Senate Agriculture Committee between 1997–2011. In that role, I helped to lead the committee's efforts in crafting provisions of the trade title in the 2002 and 2008 farm bills, and we were able to make modest reforms in the direction of improved efficiency and flexibility of the Title II ''Food for Peace'' program in both bills. Those modest reforms were continued in the 2014 farm bill passed in February of last year. The reforms to the Food for Peace program proposed in the bill introduced by the chairman and Senator Coons in February would take a giant stride further down that path.

In the 2002 farm bill, Congress first began to recognize that the traditional mode of U.S. assistance under the title II program, which consisted of purchasing and shipping U.S.-sourced commodities after a natural disaster or conflict had already occurred and people were going hungry, did not always offer the optimal response. Implementing partners reported struggling to avoid so-called pipeline breaks, during the period when the affected area had insufficient food and U.S. commodity food aid had not yet arrived. In that bill, Congress authorized the U.S. Agency for International Development (USAID) to set up warehouses to hold food aid commodities that could be quickly dispatched when emergencies arose. This greater degree of flexibility, called prepositioning, enabled the Agency to reduce the time needed to deliver assistance.

Congress expanded authority for prepositioning in the 2008 farm bill, allowing USAID to establish additional sites. The bill also increased the share of title II funding that can be used to cover certain types of nonfood expenses under Section 202(e) of the Food for Peace Act, from around 5 percent to a maximum of 13 percent. That initial bump-up in the 202(e) percentage allowed USAID to provide more cash resources to implementing partners, reducing the sale of commodities in fragile, often poorly functioning markets, a process called monetization, by about 10 percentage points. Monetization has traditionally been used to cover the nonfood components of nonemergency projects. Both provisions improved the efficiency of the program, by reducing the delivery time for food aid substantially and the cost of running development programs under title II. A recent GAO study found that using commodities stored at prepositioning warehouses cut delivery time for emergency aid by about 2 months compared to shipping directly from the United States.

The other major milestone in the 2008 farm bill was the establishment of a pilot program intended to test, in a rigorous way, what gains in efficiency might be available from allowing U.S. resources to be used to purchase food closer to where the beneficiaries are actually located, in the local area if possible or from neighboring countries if that is the closest surplus area. The legislation provided $60 million in mandatory funds for USDA to run this local and regional procurement, or LRP pilot program. Independent studies on the results of the LRP pilot found that buying locally was less expensive for most categories of commodities. Local purchases of unprocessed grain were on average 35 percent less costly, and averaged 31 percent less for unprocessed pulse crops such as peas and lentils. In addition, it was almost always more expeditious to buy locally instead of buying and shipping U.S.-sourced commodities for food aid. The emergency projects under the pilot program had an average response time of 56 days, as opposed to 130 days needed for comparable U.S.-sourced commodities to arrive at their destinations.

The 2014 farm bill moved the dial on reform further, raising the share of title II funds that can be used to cover nonfood expenses from 13 to 20 percent, and expanding the category of eligible expenses. The legislation also authorized a standing LRP program (for up to $80 million annually) to be run by USDA in part as a complement to the McGovern-Dole international school feeding program. The new program has yet to receive funding, although the President's FY16 budget proposed $20 million for that purpose.

To augment the limited flexibility available under current Food for Peace Program rules, USAID established the Emergency Food Security Program (EFSP) in 2010. It was designed to utilize LRP and other cash-based mechanisms under the broad authority of the Foreign Assistance Act. USAID now has some ability to tailor the U.S. response to the variety of circumstances under which international food assistance is needed. The steps USAID has taken in recent years have allowed the Agency to reduce the need of implementing organizations to monetize U.S. commodities under title II development projects around the world, except to meet the overall monetization minimum requirement of 15 percent that remains in effect. GAO studies in recent years indicated that monetization transactions often generated proceeds that were 76 percent or less of what was originally spent on the commodity in the United States.

This flexibility has also been crucial to addressing emergencies in places like Syria over the last few years, where it is almost impossible to safely provide U.S. food as assistance, so they have used cash assistance or food vouchers instead. However, there are some situations, such as in the Democratic Republic of Congo or the Central African Republic, where flexible resources would be helpful but are not available because of the limitations in place. S. 525 would expand that flexibility by a significant margin—I understand that USAID has estimated that the bill's increased flexibility would enable them to help about 12 million more recipients annually, which would amount to a 33-percent increase in the reach of the program compared to FY13 estimates.

I would like to point out, however, that there is no need to assume that this legislation would necessarily turn the title II program into an entirely cash-based program. We know from the results of the LRP pilot program I described earlier that there are some commodities that are cheaper to produce and ship from the United States than to purchase locally in recipient countries. This was broadly the case for vegetable oil, which on average costs $100 less per ton to buy and ship from the United States than it did to procure the same product locally. In general, the more highly processed the commodity was, the smaller the difference in cost between U.S.-sourced and foreign-sourced products. The pilot also showed that it was cheaper to buy a range of food aid commodities from the United States and ship to nearby destinations in Central and Latin America than to buy locally.

We also know that there will always be some situations where the problem is simply inadequate food for those in need in the targeted region. For those beneficiaries, sourcing U.S. food will remain the best solution. In South Sudan, for example, there has been insufficient food locally to feed the population since the most recent outbreak of civil conflict there in December 2013. As a result, USAID has provided more than $530 million in title II food aid targeting 3.2 million people over the past year and a half. No EFSP resources have been used there, because there's little food available in the region.

The Food for Peace program has been around for a long time—the program celebrated its 60th anniversary last summer, and it is estimated to have helped more than 3 billion people over that period. However, like every other U.S. agricultural policy, it needs to be modernized to better reflect the current market and policy environment as well as make use of advancements in knowledge and practice about the best approach to addressing acute and chronic food insecurity.

In its early years, the Food for Peace Program was an important component of U.S. agricultural trade policy—in 1957, it is estimated that U.S. food aid accounted for about 30 percent of all U.S. agricultural exports. Today, food aid shipments account for less than 1 percent of total U.S. agricultural exports. In fiscal 2014, U.S. food aid shipments totaled less than 1 million tons, due in large part to a combination of high commodity and transportation costs. While U.S. farmers continue to take pride in providing food for hungry people, this program is no longer viewed by the most in the agriculture sector as a key engine for expanding U.S. agricultural trade.

Another source of inefficiency in the current food aid program is the requirement that 50 percent of all U.S. food aid be shipped on U.S.-flagged vessels, otherwise known as agricultural cargo preference. One recent study by two economists from Cornell University estimated that shipping on U.S.-flagged vessels in 2006 was 46 percent more expensive than using foreign-flagged shipping. Until recently, the cost of that inefficiency was largely borne by the U.S. Department of Transportation, which was required to reimburse the food aid agencies for at least a portion of the additional costs associated with utilizing U.S-flagged shipping. However, the reimbursement requirement was repealed as part of the Bipartisan Budget Act of 2013, and now those additional costs mean that fewer hungry people can be fed with the same level of food aid resources.

If preserving military useful sealift capacity is the goal of agricultural cargo preference, it seems to me there are a lot more efficient ways to provide that support than by diverting resources intended to help the poorest people in the world. The Department of Transportation maintains a roster of 60 U.S.-flagged vessels which receive a direct annual subsidy under the Maritime Security Program (MSP) to be ready to be activated in a military emergency. However, a recent analysis conducted by a team at George Mason University found that fewer than half of the U.S.-flagged vessels which carried U.S. food aid during the period of 2011–13 were actually included in the MSP, and those ships carried only 18 percent of the food aid moved on U.S.-flagged ships on a volume basis. The other U.S.-flagged ships carrying food aid were not eligible for the MSP during that period because either they were too old or did not have the right type of shipping capacity.

Some have raised concerns about the quality of food that might be purchased locally or regionally with U.S. resources under a flexible food assistance program such as S. 525 would create. I anticipate that implementing partners would be required to monitor the quality of the food they distribute whether it is procured in the United States or abroad, as has been the case with other LRP activities conducted by the U.S. Government. In the 2008 farm bill, specific requirements for quality testing were written into the statutory language for the LRP pilot program. The study on the pilot reported few problems in meeting those requirements, with only a few defaults on contracts due to quality problems with the delivered commodities, and the rejected commodities had to be replaced at no cost to the program. The Annual Program Statement (APS) under which applications are made for both title II emergency food aid and EFSP resources requires that food products procured locally or regionally must meet the recipient country's food safety standards, and if no standards exist, they must meet international Codex Alimentarius standards instead.

For the last several decades, the United States has been the leading provider of humanitarian food assistance around the world, a position we can all take pride in. However, that assistance is still delivered primarily by a mechanism that was appropriate for the market environment at the time that the Food for Peace program was established 60 years ago, but no longer adequately meets the needs of the people the program is intended to serve. It is past time for U.S. food aid policy to enter the 21st century—Congress should allow USAID and USDA to provide the type of assistance that can be tailored to the complex environments where hungry people around the world are often found.

The CHAIRMAN. Thank you all for your testimony. I think you have all been most helpful. There are not many Americans, I realize, who watch these kinds of panels, but this panel is selected jointly by Republicans and Democrats, and it is amazing to me that the message is exactly the same by the panelists.

I want to ask a few questions and then make a statement, and then turn to our ranking member.

Dr. Smith, it is my understanding, if I heard you correctly, that 70 percent to 75 percent of the ships moving food aid are not militarily useful. Is that correct?

Dr. SMITH. The evidence in a study by Bageant, Barrett, and Lentz shows that approximately 70 percent of the vessels that move food aid are too old and/or are of a not particularly useful type for the Department of Defense to use in sealift capacity. Bulk carriers, for example, and tankers are not the ideal vessels.

Many of the vessels used in food aid are over the age that the Department of Defense identifies as being a reasonable age for shipping, and they tend to be the older, slow vessels. There really is an argument, and there is, certainly, lots of anecdotal evidence, that these ships are actually brought in to the marine fleet services of the companies that use them, these 70 percent of them that are not eligible, in order to take advantage of the food aid program reimbursements, which tend to be relatively large. These are not vessels, many of them, that would be competitive in any other way.

So effectively, this becomes a corporate welfare program for a limited number of companies, some of whom are primarily foreign-owned through holding companies.

The CHAIRMAN. It is my understanding that that number actually could be as much as 40 percent foreign-owned. Is that correct?

Dr. SMITH. That is the estimate in the literature, yes.

The CHAIRMAN. Yes. So to go down the same path we did with our former witness, first of all, food aid certainly is not designed for national security. But the fact that this actually has significant effect on our national security again is a total hoax. Is that correct? Let me say, mostly a hoax, okay? [Laughter.]

Dr. SMITH. Distinguished Chairman, I want to respond in a British House of Cards way: You might say that. Perhaps I could not.

The CHAIRMAN. I have not seen House of Cards, but I understand they say those kinds of things.

Dr. SMITH. If I may, there is a related issue. The related issue is that there is a fairly rapid growth in the intracoastal shipping that requires cargo preference for U.S. boats. There is growth there. The recent George Mason study shows that.

That growth far exceeds, on an annual basis, any loss of capacity that might be associated with moving cargo preference away from food aid cargoes.

So if you think about it this way, there are events occurring within that sector that have offsetting effects that are not related to food aid that are related to the cargo preference requirements for shipping from one U.S. port to another.

That is an important point. The 450 sailors I mentioned in my testimony, those are real people. And a legitimate question for the committee would be, would those people that lose their jobs? The answer is there is growth in shipping, in terms of the amount of product being carried? So it seems very unlikely that a change in the way in which food aid has to be shipped would cause sailors en masse, those 450 sailors, to all lose their jobs or perhaps any of them to lose their jobs. And that matters because these are real people.

The CHAIRMAN. Well, based on the amount of money we are blowing, I think you said we are spending more on shipping than on food.

Dr. SMITH. That is the GAO report evidence, yes.

The CHAIRMAN. These 450 folks could be sent to Tahiti and supported for the rest of their lives better than any of us, and we would still be saving huge amounts of money. So I think we can figure out a way to deal with that.

Dr. SMITH. Well, if you send them to Montana, Senator, that would help our population.

The CHAIRMAN. Very good.

This is for everybody. In recent years, some countries in Africa have received U.S. food aid in the form of U.S. commodities for several years in a row. Do you think this has hampered some recipients' ability to recover from the shock of the initial disaster that they faced? This is for all of you, briefly.

Dr. MERCIER. Thank you, Mr. Chairman, for the question. I think probably there are a number of reasons why some of these countries may be facing multiple years of need for assistance. Some of the times it is continuing civil conflict. Sometimes it is continued bad weather.

But I think the fact that they may even be becoming dependent on U.S. food may be hampering their ability to take steps in their own lives that would help them adjust to the changes. So I suspect that the presence of that food every year is also hampering the ability of local markets to adjust and recover from the disaster.

So in some ways, I think it does contribute.

Dr. SMITH. You have to weigh the benefits and the costs. For an economist to say that is in an inevitable thing, I know.

But the benefits are that you keep people going. And there are adjustment processes that have to take place.

The evidence on the impact, the econometric, the statistical evidence on the impact of food aid supplies on local prices is that those effects are, if there, very small in most cases. That is what the data says. That is the data-driven evidence. So that would be my comment in this context.

So that speaks to the likelihood of adversely affecting the development and production of food by smallholder farmers around the world.

Mr. RAY. As the only noneconomist on the panel, I will just speak from the point of view of an operational NGO. Our experience, certainly, suggests, if we had more flexibility, that kind of support could be provided in ways that actually helps to rebuild economies, that helps to build self-sustaining market systems in ways that help people recover more quickly and more thoroughly.

The CHAIRMAN. Listen, again, I want to thank Senator Cardin, Senator Coons, Senator Kaine, Senator Gardner, who was here earlier. I think that we have an opportunity here to work together to solve this problem.

I will say that I wish every American could have seen this testimony today. What is happening in food aid in our Nation, for a few special interests that benefit only marginally, is a national disgrace—a national disgrace. I am going to do everything in my power to make sure that every American I come in contact with is aware that a few special interests that have negligible impact, really, on them, but they have this Nation in their grip, people are dying and starving—dying and starving—because of this national disgrace of corporate welfare that is totally unnecessary, totally unnecessary to the beneficiaries.

So I thank you for being here. I look forward to working constructively with people on this committee, as we have so much recently, to ensure that our focus here is on making sure that people who are hungry have the basic food elements that they need to survive.

Thank you very much.

Ranking Member Cardin.

Senator CARDIN. Evidently, your comments brought in reinforcements. [Laughter.]

As I said earlier, I strongly support a more robust Federal budget for development assistance, including food aid. I am very disappointed that we not only have not had an increase, but we have had a decrease. We should be increasing the size of the pie going to these national security issues and furthering the policies of America. And I want to make sure that every dollar we spend is spent in the most cost-effective, efficient way. So I join the chairman, Senator Coons, and others in that regard.

I do feel, though, obligated to respond on the U.S.-flagged issue. I will be the first to acknowledge that I am not an expert on this. I do not serve on the committees that deal with this issue.

But let me just quote from the person who is responsible for that, General Paul Selva, who is the current commander in the U.S. Transportation Command who spoke directly about this issue before the Senate Committee on Armed Services on March 19 of this year. He was commenting about the reductions of cargo being used on U.S.-flagged vessels and specifically referenced the reductions in food aid.

He said, ''With the recent vessel reductions, the mariner base is at a point where future reductions in U.S.-flagged capacity puts our ability to fully activate, deploy, and sustain forces at increased risk.'' Now, that is the person who is responsible for our defense needs as to what is happening with U.S.-flagged vessels.

Now let me quote from Maj. Gen. Kathleen Gainey commenting about our merchant marines as the fourth arm of the Department of Defense and critical to the Nation.

So this is a defense issue. I agree with the chairman that food aid's purpose is not national defense from the point of view of the merchant marines. I agree with you on that. But I do think we need to know the impact it has on U.S. readiness.

The last point I would mention, quoting from the U.S. Maritime Industry, that the alternative here is to use foreign-flagged vessels for national defense, or for DOD to build, maintain, and operate the requisite vessels itself.

I just think that is an issue that we have to be mindful of. I want to make sure our programs are efficient. It is not this committee's specific charge to deal with this issue, but I do think it is a matter that we have to be mindful of as we go through these types of issues.

Let me turn my questioning, though, to an issue that we have more harmony on. I have already mentioned that there is a concern when you reduce the amount of local produced products, as far as popular support is concerned. I think that is a fact. It is something we have to deal with.

I do believe, though, there is tremendous benefit by local sourcing of agriculture in the host country. I think it gives us an opportunity to develop the type of economy that will be able to sustain itself and grow and provide for its own people. So there are a lot of advantages to local sourcing.

I also think it allows us the opportunity to deal with other goals of development assistance, and that is creating the structures within countries to make sure that they deal with corruption and deal with gender equity. In agriculture, that is a very important factor.

But when we source locally, we have the opportunity to have a more direct impact and can really make the lasting changes that can bring about stable countries that can take care of their own needs. So I think that is a real important plus for local sourcing.

I talked to former administrator Shah about this on several different occasions, as to how we can improve local capacity and build the types of structures that will be in our long-term interest.

So I just would welcome the thoughts of any of the panelists as to how we could be more effective in local sourcing to develop the type of sustainable institutions within the host countries that will give real hope for future stability and economic opportunities in these countries.

Mr. RAY. If I could just refer back to the Kore Lavi program I mentioned in my testimony, in Haiti. In that particular instance, I think it is a good example of how we are working very closely with the Haitian Government both to design the program and to build their capacity to operate that program long after we and the U.S. Government leave.

There are also secondary benefits in terms of helping to build the financial system because we are working through the formal financial system as well as building up the informal financial system through microfinance organizations.

As part of that, we are also having an effect on the agricultural industry more broadly by increasing demand for locally produced products and bringing, in this case, very purposefully more women into that value chain so that they, in fact, can continue to improve their own lot and the lot of their families and communities for many years to come.

Senator CARDIN. That is very beneficial. The gender issue is critical in these countries. Agriculture is an area where there has been huge discrimination against women.

Mr. RAY. Absolutely.

Senator CARDIN. So it seems to me that if we leverage local sourcing, we can do that with a focus to really make a lasting change, not just feeding hungry people but giving them a future of hope and a much more stable country.

Dr. MERCIER. Senator Cardin, there is another example. The World Food Programme has run a program they call Purchase for Progress, or P4P, over the last several years where they focus resources on procuring food from smallholders, from cooperatives, not from big conglomerates or multinational firms, but from small producers. And it has been very, very effective in terms of helping build capacity and building confidence among those smallholder farmers that they can produce a product and have a reliable market to be able to sell into.

So I think that is an example of the kind of things you are looking at. It is something that WFP has been working on and perfecting for several years now.

Senator CARDIN. Mr. Chairman, I was very pleased to hear from the previous witness about steps they are taking to deal with corruption, because I am very worried about corruption and the efficiency of our programs.

It does seem to me that the reforms that you are working on really will give us a better opportunity to deal with these problems in-country, not just providing food but providing a way in which they can have a sustainable future. I think the way the program is being administered from the anticorruption angle is a huge step forward.

The CHAIRMAN. Thank you. Thank you so much for your input and just tremendous successes we have had recently.

Senator Perdue.

Senator PERDUE. Thank you, Mr. Chairman.

Thank you, folks, for being here this morning.

Having lived outside the United States, I have witnessed the benefits of what you guys do and I want to applaud what you do, and especially the operation CARE being based in Georgia.

I am very proud, Mr. Ray, that you are here.

Dr. Mercier, I have just a couple questions. From the business sector and business perspective, your recommendations about increasing efficiency, what reforms and what benefits could those reforms bring to the U.S. agriculture business? And how can that help provide for the needs that we are trying to meet in the programs that you guys are representing? Talk about our port systems and national security, as well as shipping.

As part of that, my observation is that one of the problems we have in these host countries that we are trying to ship to is infrastructure.

Our State exports to a lot of poultry. One of the problems you have is you can get it to their ports. Once it gets to the port, it is very difficult to distribute within the countries. So protein, fat, sugar, those things are in high demand there.

Can you just speak to some of those issues as we look at this?

Dr. MERCIER. Yes. I think what you are getting at goes far beyond what international food aid really provides, and that is a broader international ag development effort. I have seen food aid as being the starting point of U.S. assistance.

You have a region of a country where there is a drought or civil conflict, people just do not have enough food, and you try to figure out what is the optimal response for meeting that emergency need. But you also think beyond that, to some extent, as to how you help that population transition into being more self-sufficient, building up the infrastructure.

So one of the things that I think is an important development in recent years is the recognition that you need to try to build resiliency in those local populations. So you need to have a combination of instruments and programs that help them do that. Part of that is making sure they have enough food when they are really hungry and that is largely a food aid issue.

But beyond that, it is international development. It is helping them get seed. It is helping them build roads. It is helping, as in the case of the poultry exports, build capacity at the ports so they can have some cold storage, so they can actually utilize U.S. or other sources of protein.

So it is a combination. There are a number of institutions within USAID, not just the Office of Food for Peace, but also the Bureau for Food Security, who are focusing on making these kinds of opportunities available to these folks.

Senator PERDUE. Thank you, Mr. Chairman.

The CHAIRMAN. Senator Coons.

Senator COONS. Thank you, Chairman Corker, for convening this and leading this effort.

Thank you, Senator Cardin, for your insight and your questions.

I want to pursue three lines of inquiry, if I might.

First, on monetization. David, I want to commend CARE and you for giving up what is tens of millions of dollars of potential cash for CARE in recognition, if I understood your testimony correctly, that there are harmful effects to monetization, that is not just inefficient, it also, in some instances, has been documented to have a negative impact on resiliency and on the development of markets in some of the countries we are most trying to help.

Why does monetization continue as a practice? What would be the potential benefits and how might we structure a reduction to monetization and offset it with a more efficient and responsible practice for supporting NGOs, whose primary purpose is providing relief to those who are struggling with food insecurity?

Mr. RAY. Senator, thank you for your question and for your recognition.

There are a couple of reasons that monetization continues. Perhaps the most concrete one is that it is required by law. Fifteen percent of the——

Senator COONS. This is leading up to my question about reforms we could make by law.

Mr. RAY. Right. So 15 percent of title II nonemergency funds are required to be monetized, and so they are.

But on a practical level, there are organizations who continue to monetize because it supports very important ongoing development programs. If, in fact, that money was made available as cash, then we would not have to monetize and we could be actually getting a hundred percent of the value of those dollars rather than $.70 or less on the dollar, and actually do more good.

The CHAIRMAN. Senator Coons, if I could, could I add a minute or 2 to your time, and for people who are just watching this, ask your witness to explain how monetization works?

Senator COONS. Sure.

The CHAIRMAN. I think it would be helpful to everyone and help build a case for what you are trying to——

Senator COONS. If you would, please, because once you really grasp what monetization is and how it works, it is hard to see it as an admirable practice.

I am not meaning to impugn those NGOs who benefit from monetization.

Mr. RAY. Not at all.

Senator COONS. They provide valued and needed services. But the inefficiency of it really is striking.

So, Mr. Ray, if you could?

Mr. RAY. As I mentioned in my testimony, monetization, very simply put, is the practice of buying commodities here, shipping them to developing countries, selling them there, often at a loss, and then using those proceeds to fund long-term development programs.

Certainly, our argument has been that it would be a much more efficient and effective way to fund those programs to just supply the money rather than go through that very convoluted method and, in fact, losing money on the whole transaction.

Senator COONS. And in the same spirit, Dr. Smith, you testified somewhat about the sealift, the maritime fleet that is sustained through cargo preference. Senator Cardin shared some important testimony in front of the Armed Services Committee that suggested that sealift remains an important priority for our national security.

You testified earlier that there is a significant mismatch, that a lot of the fleet that is being used for food aid really is not helpful or relevant for maritime military sealift. If we were to simply more directly fund through DOD the maintenance of a DOD appropriate sealift capacity, what difference might there be in efficiency of outcome?

Dr. SMITH. I have not run those numbers, and I have not seen a clear number.

Senator COONS. A rough impression.

Dr. SMITH. A rough impression is, let us have a program that has one goal, not that is diverted to a program that has another goal.

Senator COONS. Right.

Dr. SMITH. That is the fundamental message.

If DOD thought the expansion of capacity was important on a maritime basis, then DOD should be making the decisions about allocating funds there. But if I am a general or admiral or even a Senator with issues associated with maritime shipping, I would really like someone else to have to pay for those costs, rather than use my chits.

That is really what we are seeing. We are seeing a litany, if you like, or almost a liturgy, from the maritime interests that say this is a vital piece of support. If you look at the dollars, the amount of dollars that actually go to the maritime private sector from food aid are much smaller on a per ship basis than $3.1 million annually than currently ships qualified as a DOD ready for shipment are currently getting.

There is a complete mismatch there. The problem, of course, is that all of the funds that come out of food aid into shipping reduce the capacity of the food aid programs at current funding levels to deal with genuine human tragedy. And that is what is really problematic.

It is not problematic that the Department of Defense wants to make sure they have adequate resources to protect this Nation. And it is not problematic—if I owned a ship, I would want cargo preference, too. We understand profit incentives.

Senator COONS. Understood. So that brings me to my last question, which I think is really the key question here, Dr. Mercier. And the whole panel might address this.

So we are using food aid partly to provide food aid, and partly to provide relief from food insecurity, and partly to sustain sealift capacity, and partly to sustain maritime labor, and partly to provide monetization support for NGOs.

The concern that has always been raised in these conversations is, what would the impact be if we significantly streamlined and modernized this program so that DOD is paying for sealift and we are providing direct support for NGOs that are doing important development work? And where it is appropriate, we are buying

U.S. commodities and shipping them on Jones Act ships and delivering them with American labor. And where it is not, we are doing direct, flexible, local procurement or direct provision through electronic means, as you testified.

How would we sustain food aid? How vital are these sectors to sustaining the allocation of food aid?

Senator Cardin raised this central point. The appropriations for food aid have gone down in recent years. I would love to hear from all three of you, what is your guesstimate of the impact on food aid for the long-term, if we were, in fact, to make it more efficient?

Dr. MERCIER. Thank you for the question, Senator Coons. This is an issue that was of great concern for me when I worked on the Agriculture Committee. Sort of what I worked through over the years is that you need to maintain a balance, and I think it is important to recognize, just based on the LRP pilot program, that there is going to be continuing need to purchase U.S. commodities for use in these programs.

In some cases, it is going to be because it is more cost effective. That is largely the case with the more value-added commodities, processed products, vegetable oil, that kind of thing. It is still going to be more cost effective to buy here and ship it overseas. That is especially the case for nearby destinations like in Central America or Latin America.

Then there are some places where there is just simply not enough food, and we need to supplement that with U.S. commodities.

So this is going to continue to be a program that uses U.S. food. It just needs to be one that has other mechanisms available as well.

The maritime issues, I recognize that this is a legitimate national security objective, to provide assurance of having that sealift capacity in the need of emergency, but I do not think this is a cost-effective way of doing it, as Dr. Smith mentioned. The data suggests that a lot of the ships carrying food aid are not suited for that reason.

Senator COONS. I am out of time. My question is not about cost-effectiveness. I think we have discussed in great detail how cost inefficient this is.

My question is about whether or not the NGO community and the good intentions of the American people are enough to sustain food aid at its current levels or higher, or whether these other communities of interest have to be engaged in order to sustain food aid?

Any opinions from Mr. Ray or Dr. Smith would be welcome as well.

Dr. SMITH. Let me speak to the agricultural sector, because a lot of my work is on agriculture.

There is a clear case to be made that American farmers actually will benefit by more efficient use of current dollars because it essentially increases global demand for these key commodities, wheat, corn, rice, and so on.

There is a paradox here. The litany has always been wrong here, that the notion that you have to buy American for American farmers to benefit is simply wrong. If we take the crude economic view that what they care about is the price of wheat or the price of corn or the price of peanut butter, what matters is how much is being taken off the global market in these globally traded commodities.

I think that is the case that a wide array of supporters of food aid should make. I think they are also shooting from the hip with no expertise in this area at all.

There are things that we can do to make it clear to the American farmer that their work is critical to feeding the world. For example, where possible, stamping all food aid delivered in bulk as provided with the support of the American farmer is a very nice way to go, where that is politically appropriate. Things like that are important in sustaining effort.

It is unclear to me that the mercantile service is really an important factor in overall development aid here. It is unclear to me what they are doing. It seems to me, to be honest, that the private maritime interests are lobbying for their corporate welfare.

And there is an issue about assuring adequate capacity for the marine fleet to support DOD efforts. There are other ways to go that are more efficient, and I am going to stop there because I am not an expert in how politically you form those alliances that help them get more money in other directions that would be efficient, but less money than they are currently taking out from the cargo preference approach.

Senator COONS. Mr. Chairman, do you want to let Mr. Ray answer the question?

The CHAIRMAN. Sure.

Mr. RAY. Thank you. If I may, Senator, I think you bring up really critical points and something that, certainly, has been of concern to us. The last thing we want to do is see support for these vital programs reduced.

I will, however, say this, as an organization with 1 million supporters around the country and 250,000 members of our citizen advocacy network in every district and State around the country, our experience has been that the most effective way to build support for foreign assistance programs, and for this program, in particular, is for it to be as effective and efficient as possible.

If we can deliver on that, we will generate public support for this program. I am confident we can retain the level of public support that will provide political support and backing to Members of Congress to continue to fund this program.

Senator COONS. Thank you. Thank you, Mr. Ray.

Thank you to the whole panel for your testimony.

Thank you, Mr. Chairman.

The CHAIRMAN. Thank you.

Senator Coons, thank you for asking the great question about what if food aid were focused on food aid. That would be a good thing.

I would just say, editorially, I doubt there are other aid programs that we participate in that have such a small amount of corporate welfare interests that cause us to waste as much money. I just cannot believe 450 sailors are generating the support for this aid program. And I just hope that we will figure out a way to deal appropriately with it.

Senator Shaheen.

Senator SHAHEEN. Thank you, Mr. Chairman, and thank you to you and Senator Coons for this legislation, and to all of the panelists for not only your testimony this morning, but for your great work in helping to provide food aid to people around the world.

You know, I share the sentiments that have already been expressed, that it is very important for us to look at the budget for food aid and try to increase that, but that we also need to be as efficient as possible, and that there are a lot of things about the current program that do not seem to work in a way that is understandable for the American people.

I share your point, Mr. Ray. I think people want what government does to be effective and efficient. And if we can make that case, it is much easier to get support for the programs the government provides.

I had a couple specific questions that have come up as a result of Senator Cardin's question and raising the concerns about the maritime industry. Does anybody know—and maybe you know this, Senator Cardin—what percentage of cargo that is shipped by the U.S. maritime industry is actually food aid?

Dr. Mercier.

Dr. MERCIER. Yes. There are three kinds of cargo that are affected by cargo preference rules. The biggest by far is military cargo. So it is tanks. It is fuel. It is the kind of things that we need our military overseas to have access to. That is about 86 percent of it. Food aid is about 6 to 8 percent. And then the remainder is material that is shipped out under transactions by U.S. Import-Export Bank, those kinds of things.

So food aid is a very, very small share of what is covered by cargo preference right now.

Senator SHAHEEN. Is there a dollar amount that accounts for that, or a percentage of income of the U.S. maritime industry that can be attributed to food aid?

Dr. Smith.

Dr. SMITH. A group at George Mason has estimated that less than 1 percent of the total value of cargo that is carried by the maritime fleet, either commercially or under cargo preference, is food aid. And the followup is you always have to remember that the majority of that amount that is being shipped is being shipped on ships that are not included in the DOD assessment of military preparedness.

Senator CARDIN. Senator, would you yield just for 1 minute so I can get Dr. Mercier to just comment?

Senator SHAHEEN. Sure.

Senator CARDIN. As we are winding down our military operations, would the percentage of food aid increase since we are now transporting less military?

Dr. MERCIER. I suppose that is possible, but the tonnage that is being shipped under food aid is also declining over time. As recently as 5 years ago, we were talking 4 million or 5 million tons of food aid, and I think over the last couple years, it has been about 2 million tons.

So both numbers are going down, and so I am not sure the relative shares are going to be changing that much.

Dr. SMITH. And just to come back to a point that was made earlier; in 2002, corn was selling at $2.20 a bushel. Today, it is selling at $3.80. And the budget available for food aid has not changed measurably at all.

So a ton of corn, a ton of wheat, costs more money for reasons that are probably not germane here but do not trivially relate to ethanol.

Senator SHAHEEN. We do not want to go into that here right now. [Laughter.]

We can talk about sugar though. I am happy to talk about sugar. Sorry.

Again, I apologize for missing your testimony, so some of you may have addressed this. But in 2008, the farm bill authorized a pilot project for local and regional procurement. Do we have a report or data from what that pilot program showed us? And can any of you comment on that?

Dr. MERCIER. I think I can comment on that because I helped write the language for the provision. There has actually been a couple different reports that have been studying the results of the pilot program. One was specifically required under the statutory language and then a separate one was done by a consortium of NGOs and Cornell University. And pretty broadly what they showed is that for most commodities, when you have the cost of the commodity, plus the cost of shipping it from the United States as compared to the cost of buying it locally; you are saving anywhere between 30 to 50 percent by buying it locally. There are a couple of exceptions, which I mentioned in my testimony, vegetable oil being one.

And the other important main finding in both studies is that it is much faster to do it when you procure locally. I think the average was 130 days to ship from the United States to recipients and about 56 days, so less than half the time, if you procure locally for the emergency projects at least.

Senator SHAHEEN. So who is the second country, in terms of providing the most food aid around the world, to the United States? Does anyone know?

Dr. SMITH. Senator, we can get that information to your office very quickly. A wild guess is that it is going to be a combination, in the developed world, of Australia, Canada, and various European Union countries.

Senator SHAHEEN. That would have been my guess.

Dr. SMITH. But China is doing a lot, and that is why I want to say I will look that up for you.

Senator SHAHEEN. Okay. And can you also speak to how they provide food aid? Is it similar to what we do in the United States? Or do they more of the local and regional procurement?

Dr. MERCIER. Most of the aid provided by other donor countries is cash-based. Canada still does a mixture but I think it is predominantly cash-based. They still do some Canadian-sourced commodities, but most of the rest of the world has given their NGOs the flexibility that is being proposed in this legislation for the United States.

Senator SHAHEEN. And finally, Senator Coons raised this issue, but there are vested interests who benefit from the way the current system operates. So where is the most opposition coming from to changing the way the current system works?

Dr. SMITH. I would defer to the distinguished Chair of this committee, but a good guess is the maritime interests have been very aggressive.

Senator SHAHEEN. Certainly, we have heard from the maritime interests. Are there others?

Dr. SMITH. Some NGOs are concerned about losing their ability to compete for the cash. Whether that is any sort of a good reason for changing the system is entirely another matter. In fact, it sounds to me like the worst possible reason or among the worst possible reasons.

Senator SHAHEEN. And several of you alluded to farmers. I have not heard from any farmers in New Hampshire that they are concerned about changing the way food aid works, but they are probably not benefiting a lot from the current program. So where are farmers on these changes?

Dr. SMITH. It depends on who is speaking. That is critically——

Senator SHAHEEN. When you say that, you mean who is speaking for the farmers or who represents the farm industry?

Dr. SMITH. Yes, it depends on which lobby you are going to listen to. Perspectives have changed, though. In 1956, the corn growers and wheat growers would have been extremely supportive of food aid. They would have seen it as a major source of the demand for their product.

Today, it is a trivial proportion of the total global demand for wheat and corn, for example. And we compete in global markets, not local markets.

If anything, making reforms that would take more corn, more wheat, more rice, more peanut butter, off the market would be beneficial for those groups.

And an important issue, as I alluded to earlier, is that it is true that you want the American farm community to believe that it is making a significant contribution to helping genuine problems. Most farmers are good people.

Senator SHAHEEN. I believe that.

Dr. SMITH. Some maybe not, but most. No, overwhelmingly the farmers I know are genuine people who want to make a living, but they also recognize the importance of what they do globally. So it is important to communicate the American productivity at the farm level is a major contributor to our ability as a global community to feed the world, and to recognize their contributions in some way. But it does not have to be through sourcing wheat in Ekalaka, MT, which is in the middle of nowhere—trust me, I have been there—or anywhere in Iowa.

Senator SHAHEEN. Mr. Chairman, can I ask the other two to respond to that?

The CHAIRMAN. Sure.

Dr. MERCIER. Senator Shaheen, we actually had a concrete example in 2013 after the President made his proposal. There was actually an amendment in the House to the farm bill that would have implemented a lot of things he proposed. There was a floor vote on this issue. I was involved with consulting with NGO community at that point.

We found the most effective opposition came from the maritime industry and the associated labor unions. Agriculture, as far as we were able to tell, did not really engage very actively for the most part. There were a few exceptions. We believe the rice industry was involved to some extent. But most of them had much higher priorities in that farm bill, as they usually do.

Senator SHAHEEN. Thank you.

Mr. Ray.

Mr. RAY. I would just say, from the NGO perspective, there has been substantial support among the NGO sector for these kinds of food aid reforms. In fact, in the lead-up to this hearing, 28 NGOs signed a letter of support for the kind of food aid reform that Senators Corker and Coons have proposed.

There are, of course, concerns around the issue of monetization, but I think we have already spoken to that issue.

Senator SHAHEEN. Right.

Thank you very much.

The CHAIRMAN. Anybody else have any closing questions or comments?

I want to thank all of you for being here. I think this testimony has been outstanding, as has the hearing.

My guess is, to follow up on Dr. Smith's comments, I would bet that while there are associations and entities that lobby on behalf of various industries, if you will, I would bet if the members themselves were aware of the negative impact this lobbying was having on people who were starving, I do not believe there would be as much lobbying taking place.

I do not think they have any idea that there are paid lobbyists up here that are causing people around the world to starve. I just have greater faith in the American people, greater faith that if these groups they are representing, if the individuals actually knew what was happening, they would be ashamed and they would cause it to stop.

So I thank you all for being here.

Mr. Ray, thank you for the example your organization is setting.

Dr. Mercier, thank you for all your efforts through the years to cause reforms to happen.

The meeting will be adjourned, although for questions, the record will remain open through the end of the day Friday.

Thank you all for being here.

[Whereupon, at 11:16 a.m., the hearing was adjourned.]

ADDITIONAL MATERIAL SUBMITTED FOR THE RECORD

WRITTEN STATEMENT OF REV. DAVID BECKMANN, PRESIDENT, BREAD FOR THE WORLD

I appreciate the opportunity to submit written testimony on a subject very close to my own heart and a prime policy interest of Bread for the World.

My name is David Beckmann, president of Bread for the World, a collective Christian voice urging our Nation's decisionmakers to end hunger at home and abroad. Our network of thousands of individual members, churches, and denominations ensures Bread's presence in all U.S. congressional districts. Through the support of these members around the country and in partnership with faith groups and churches, we have worked for over 40 years to help ensure that no person faces the burden of food insecurity.

The dimensions of global hunger are well known: More than 805 million people— or one in every nine people globally. Poor nutrition causes nearly half (45 percent) of deaths in children under 5, approximately 3.1 million children each year. For such demeaning hunger and poverty to persist when we have the technological and economic means of ending it is a moral affront to American values.

Food aid has been an important tool in combating global hunger, and has saved many lives. The United States can rightly feel proud of its role as the world's most generous donor of food aid. Our efforts have saved millions of lives. However, with changes in technology and transportation, it is time to modernize food aid to create a faster and more flexible program to help eradicate hunger

The food aid environment has changed significantly from when Food for Peace was initiated over 50 years ago. Changes in the food aid program are overdue. Any food aid reform efforts should include the following.

First, increased flexibility to deliver food aid in the best way possible. Current law requires nearly all of food aid to be commodities produced in the United States. Commodity food aid is not always the most appropriate response to food insecurity, whether chronic or emergency. One life-affecting consideration is that of timeliness, ensuring the quickest response to emergencies or windows of opportunity. Other considerations include market impact—whether the commodity food aid serves as an incentive or disincentive to local or regional production and commerce—and commodity composition—i.e., whether the needs are best served by commodities or products available from the United States.

In order to facilitate the most effective and efficient responses to food insecurity, Bread for the World strongly supports allowing both U.S. and locally or regionally procured (LRP) commodities, vouchers, and cash transfers to be used. Two independent evaluations by the Government Accountability Office and a congressionally mandated study by Management Systems International found that local and regional procurement (LRP) programs have an average cost-saving of at least 25 percent compared with similar in-kind food aid programs. In some cases, these savings can increase to over 50 percent, as a Cornell University study documented, along with a 62-percent gain in timeliness of delivery. Local and regional procurement, and vouchers or cash transfers are not going to be appropriate in every case and need to be carefully applied, but there is already sufficient information and experience to clearly demonstrate the circumstances under which this instrument can be effectively applied.

Second, we support loosening the restrictions that mandate the processing ("value added") of food aid and U.S.-flag shipping. While these reflect legitimate interests, our main focus should be on meeting needs and saving lives, and employing the most appropriate and efficient means to that end. Surely, other means can be found for ensuring the viability of the U.S. merchant marine than by imposing onerous and costly restrictions on the shipment of food to meet the urgent nutritional needs of hungry people around the world.

Finally, we would like to eliminate the process of monetization. With some food aid, food is donated to a poor country and then sold there. The revenue is used to fund projects carried out by private charities or intergovernmental organizations. Unfortunately, a recent GAO study found monetization loses an average of 25 cents on every taxpayer dollar spent, and according to USAID, eliminating monetization could feed an additional 800,000 people and free up an estimated $30 million per year.

God is moving in our time to overcome hunger and poverty around the world. The world has reduced poverty and hunger; extreme poverty has been cut in half and 100 million people have escaped from hunger in just the past decade alone. Undeniably, U.S. food assistance has played a leading role in achieving these results. Yet, clearly there is more we can do, and we have the obligation and the opportunity to end hunger. We need to take advantage of every means for doing so.

Moreover, in difficult budget circumstances, when all programs must be justified, proposals to increase cost-effectiveness, save time and costs, and potentially reach more people should be strongly considered. The changes to the food aid program noted above will, I am confident, move the United States closer, in concert with the NGO community, intergovernmental organizations and other donors, toward meeting this urgent objective.

WRITTEN STATEMENT FROM THE U.S. MARITIME INDUSTRY

April 15, 2015

The Honorable Bob Corker, Chairman
Committee on Foreign Relations
United States Senate
Washington, DC 20510

The Honorable Ben Cardin, Ranking
Committee on Foreign Relations
United States Senate
Washington, DC 20510

RE: Committee Hearing on *American Food Aid: Why Reform*

Dear Mr. Chairman and Ranking Member Cardin:

On behalf of the undersigned United States-flag shipping companies, maritime associations and American maritime labor organizations, we are submitting this statement in conjunction with your Committee's hearing on *American Food Aid: Why Reform*. The United States-flag shipping companies we represent, along with our affiliated maritime labor unions who represent ships' Masters, Licensed Deck and Engineering Officers, and unlicensed merchant mariners help guarantee that the Department of Defense (DOD) will continue to have the commercial sealift capability it needs to support America's troops and to protect America's interests abroad.

At the outset, we believe it is important to note that one key component of U.S. maritime policy that promotes the use of U.S.-flag vessels and enhances the economic and security interests of the United States are the U.S.-flag cargo preference statutes. Taken together, these statutes require that a percentage of U.S. government cargoes, including United States food aid cargoes, be transported on U.S.-flag vessels if such vessels are available at fair and reasonable rates. They provide U.S.-flag vessels with a critical base of cargo, giving those vessels the opportunity to stay active while they work to compete against lower-cost and oftentimes tax-free foreign flag vessels for the carriage of commercial cargoes in the U.S. foreign trades. This in turn helps to ensure that the U.S.-flag vessels and their American crews remain available to DOD in time of war or other international emergency.

We also wish to emphasize that our U.S.-flag shipping companies, American maritime labor unions and related maritime associations understand and appreciate the need to review America's food aid programs. However, we strongly urge that any proposal to reform or revise the PL 480 Food for Peace Program, our nation's most successful foreign aid food assistance program, must ensure that the militarily-useful U.S.-flag commercial vessels, American maritime jobs and worldwide logistical networks available to our nation through the Maritime Security Program (MSP), our nation's most important commercial sealift capability program, are not adversely affected or lost. Unfortunately, S. 525, the "Food for Peace Reform Act of 2015", does not adequately address the impact that the complete elimination of the U.S.-flag shipping requirements from the Food for Peace Program will have on MSP and the U.S.-flag maritime industry.

In fact, eliminating the U.S,-flag shipping requirement for U.S. food aid cargoes will diminish our nation's U.S.-flag sealift capability and will result in the loss of American jobs. In 2011, then-Commander of the Department of Defense's Transportation Command General Duncan McNabb told Congress that "The movement of international food aid has been a major contributor to the cargo we have moved under the cargo preference law that our U.S. commercial sealift industry depends on." He warned that "Any reductions will have to be offset in other ways to maintain current DOD readiness."

Today, because of reductions in the size of the U.S.-flag fleet, DOD's commercial sealift capabilities are in peril. In fact, General Paul Selva, the current Commander of the United States Transportation Command, spoke directly on this issue in testimony to the Senate Committee on Armed Services on March 19, 2015, stating:

> "The reduction in government-impelled cargoes due to the drawdown
> in Afghanistan and reductions in food aid . . . are driving vessel owners
> to reflag to non-U.S.-flag out of economic necessity . . . With the recent vessel
> reductions, the mariner base is at the point where future reductions in
> U.S.-flag capacity puts our ability to fully activate, deploy and sustain forces
> at increased risk."

Significantly, it is the privately-owned U.S.-flag maritime industry that is called upon by DOD to deliver the supplies and equipment needed to support our troops and their mission overseas. In fact, since 2009, U.S.-flag commercial vessels crewed by civilian American merchant mariners have transported more than 90 percent of the sustainment cargo in support of the U.S. military operations and rebuilding programs in Afghanistan and Iraq. Vessels enrolled in the MSP carried 99 percent of these cargoes.

The role played by our privately-owned U.S.-flag maritime industry can be best illustrated by the comments made in 2008 by Major General Kathleen Gainey, Commander, U.S. Military Surface Deployment and Distribution Command. She stated that "The merchant marine has always been there beside us . . . You have been there and delivered for our service members around the world . . . I am here to tell you, having deployed twice, I know how critical it is that we get that equipment and supplies on time . . . You are the fourth arm of the Department of Defense and you are critical to this nation."

Proposals that are put forward to modify the nature of the Food for Peace Program and its implementation in order to meet changing international food aid assistance needs and requirements must recognize that many such changes will have an impact on U.S.-flag commercial sealift capability. This capability – the U.S.-flag vessels, the worldwide logistics networks provided by MSP vessel operators, and the U.S. citizen mariners who crew the government and private vessels that provide surge and sustainment capabilities for DOD – is available to DOD to supply and support American troops overseas and to respond in time of war or other international emergency.

Diminishing this capability through changes in the food aid programs means that our country will either have to rely on foreign flag vessels and foreign mariners for advancing America's security interests and supporting American troops abroad, or that DOD must build, maintain and operate the requisite vessels itself. Most importantly, diminishing this capability through changes in the food aid programs will result in the significant reduction in the active pool of experienced civilian U.S. mariners available to crew the Military Sealift Command's and Maritime Administration's surge fleet as well as the privately-owned commercial sustainment fleet when required to meet national defense objectives. As stated in a March 20, 2015 letter to the Appropriations Committee highlighting the importance of MSP and the need to maintain the capability it provides, Senators Roger Wicker, Cory Booker and eight of their colleagues noted that the first option – relying on foreign vessels and crews – "would result in the outsourcing of American maritime jobs as we spend taxpayer dollars on foreign flag ships and crews who may not share America's goals and interests" and that the second option "would cost the government at least $65 billion to replicate the capacity provided by [MSP]vessels . . ."

We understand the United States Agency for International Development, the Department of Transportation and its Maritime Administration, the Department of Agriculture and others within the Administration are working together to craft a proposal that would reform the Food for Peace Program and enhance America's commercial sealift capability. We are encouraged by their efforts and are hopeful that we can move past the in-fighting that has defined the food aid reform debate for the past several years. If a compromise agreement can be reached that ensures the long-term support of the U.S.-flag ships and American mariners needed to meet military needs, extends the reach and effectiveness of emergency food assistance programs, and maintains an important role for U.S. agricultural commodities, we think it would enjoy broad-based support in Congress and among the affected stakeholders.

We look forward to working with you and your colleagues in support of legislation that both reforms the Food for Peace Program and enhances the U.S.-flag commercial sealift capability provided through MSP. We stand ready to discuss this issue with you and your staff in more detail at your convenience.

We ask that this statement be included in your Committee's hearing record on *American Food Aid: Why Reform.*

Sincerely,

American Maritime Congress
American Maritime Officers
American Maritime Officers Services
APL Maritime Ltd.
American Roll-on Roll-off Carrier
Central Gulf Lines, Inc.
Hapag Lloyd USA, LLC
International Organization of Masters, Mates & Pilots
Maersk Line, Limited
Marine Engineers' Beneficial Association
Marine Firemen's Union
Maritime Institute for Research and Industrial Development
Maritime Trades Department, AFL-CIO
Sailors' Union of the Pacific
Seafarers International Union
Transportation Institute
Transportation Trades Department, AFL-CIO
Waterman Steamship Corporation

Written Statement of Mercy Corps

On behalf of Mercy Corps, an Oregon-based humanitarian and development non-profit organization, we would like to thank the chairman for his deep commitment to food aid reform and for holding this important hearing. Mercy Corps works in over 40 countries around the world. We are dedicated to alleviating suffering, poverty and oppression by helping people build secure, productive, and just communities. A major foundation of our work is in helping communities' increase their food security; Mercy Corps' agricultural programs are valued today at more than USD $200 million and implemented in 27 countries.

Mercy Corps supports the chairman's and committee's continued efforts to reform U.S. food aid programs to make them more efficiently help the world's most vulnerable people. We would like to offer the following testimony that highlights the urgent need for reform in title II emergency and nonemergency programs, the importance of building resilience in the developing world and provide recommendations to the committee for additional steps to take to continue to support food aid reform.

LOCAL AND REGIONAL PROCUREMENT AND THE USE OF CASH IN EMERGENCY RESPONSES

With unprecedented emergencies around the world and limited resources to respond to these crises, it has never been more important to encourage innovations that improve emergency food aid. Local and Regional Procurement (LRP) is the purchase of food aid in the country or region of distribution, or the use of cash and/or vouchers for the purchase of food and/or nonfood items that reduce food insecurity among the targeted population.

Mercy Corps has been a leader in researching and implementing LRP. Our research has found that LRP is more efficient, cost-effective and has a high impact. Specifically, LRP provides:

- Efficiencies: LRP ensures hungry and malnourished people receive food quickly. While U.S. commodities can take 4 to 6 months to arrive to the implementing organization, the average time for Mercy Corps' LRP programs to procure commodities was just over 1 month. This means LRP can ensure essential food assistance reaches those who are hungry and malnourished more than 70 percent faster than food aid provided through international commodity shipment.
- Cost Effectiveness: LRP maximizes the number of people reached with each dollar of assistance. A cost comparison of comparable goods showed that in Central Asia and Africa, Mercy Corps' LRP programs cost an average of 27 percent less than programs based on shipment of U.S. commodities.
- High Impact: LRP ensures food assistance programs enhance food security and sustainable development. Research found Mercy Corps' LRP programs are effective at improving the food security of those targeted for assistance, both immediately and in the longer term. Beneficiaries reported that LRP programs enhanced their psychological well-being, and helped families to avoid negative coping mechanisms, such as selling off productive assets to feed their families in times of crisis. By ensuring beneficiaries are able to gain access to the foods they traditionally eat, LRP programs may yield greater nutritional benefits. Private sector vendors reported that LRP programs helped them to expand businesses, build their own capacity, and integrate into formal systems, leading to more rapid and sustainable economic recovery.[1]

We would therefore recommend the committee support efforts to allow for significantly increasing flexibility within title II emergency programs to allow for more LRP and the use of cash and vouchers in emergencies. This increased flexibility would allow for the U.S. Government to reach millions of more vulnerable populations at no additional cost to the taxpayer.

THE IMPORTANCE OF NON-EMERGENCY PROGRAMS AND ENDING MONETIZATION

There are over 800 million people around the globe that do not have enough food to eat. In our decades of experience, one of the most effective programs we have seen to promote food security and address the underlying causes of hunger is the Title II Food for Peace Non-Emergency programs. These multiyear programs are an essential tool to helping communities build their resilience to crises and over time, decrease the need for emergency, lifesaving interventions. Addressing root causes of hunger so that the world's most vulnerable can rise out of poverty is a cornerstone of nonemergency programs.

Yet nonemergency programs, as originally codified in 1954, included a heavy reliance on the practice of monetization, the conversion of U.S. commodities to cash by selling them in overseas markets. Money from the sale of U.S. commodities are made available to fund program costs, like buying scales to weigh infants to ensure they gain weight properly or fund trainings for smallholder farmers in how to improve their yields. While the programmatic use of the funds gained from monetization is extremely helpful in building the capacity of communities to fight hunger, the actual practice of monetization is—the vast majority of the time—extremely inefficient. From costs lost in shipping U.S. commodities on U.S.-flagships, to shipping food inland to the point of sale, to storing the food, then organizing the actual sale of the food on the open market, monetization takes time and money. Moreover, the market prices available in other countries for the commodities sold through monetization can often be lower than the total investment that the U.S. Government has made in purchasing and shipping the food. The Government Accountability Office's 2011 report, ''Funding Development Projects through the Purchase, Shipment, and Sale of U.S. Commodities Is Inefficient and Can Cause Adverse Market Impacts'' found that USAID's average cost recovery was 76 percent, while

USDA's was 58 percent. In addition, USAID could not guarantee that the sale of commodities did not have an adverse effect on the local markets.[2]

From our personal experiences with monetization, we often face considerable setbacks including food that spoils in transit that cannot be sold, or in the case of the Democratic Republic of Congo, a monopoly by one buyer of wheat, who drives down the price of the commodity we are trying to monetize, further decreasing funds we can use of programs. Of particular frustration to our staff is that in order to program effectively, we need to know how much funds we will receive in advance from monetization so we can plan out activities over the following 6 months to a year. With monetization though, the amount of cash we will actually receive for food security programs can be radically different than what was planned for or needed.

Eliminating the need to monetize and providing cash directly to implementing partners for programmatic purposes would be vastly more efficient. Any efforts by the committee to eliminate the need to monetize would be greatly appreciated, including working to increase the amount of overall cash flexibility in title II programs to eliminating the provision in the 2014 Farm Bill that requires at least 15 percent of nonemergency funding be monetized. In FY 2015, we would also appreciate the committee's attention to ensuring sufficient cash (like from the Community Development Fund, appropriated out of the State and Foreign Operations Subcommittee) is available for nonemergency programs so that programs that were not supposed to monetize are not suddenly forced to monetize mid-year, which could dramatically impact our programs and beneficiaries.

BUILDING RESILIENCE WITH FLEXIBLE FUNDING MECHANISMS IN NON-EMERGENCY PROGRAMS

Addressing the root causes of food insecurity will require USAID, USDA, and implementers to break out of traditional "siloes" and link food security to other development challenges, including governance, conflict mitigation and peace-building. For example, in Karamoja, Northern Uganda, where 12.5 percent of children face acute malnutrition,[3] a major underlying factor contributing to food insecurity is lack of land tenure. If we are to comprehensively address hunger, we need the flexibility to analyze and respond to what the drivers of food insecurity are on the ground, including supporting efforts of smallholder farmers to gain access to land and the legal sector. While this may appear like a governance issue, it actually is a food security related activity and needs to be addressed if we are to tackle the drivers of hunger. The current authorities outline in existing legislation (the 2014 Farm Bill and underlying statute) for nonemergency programs allows for this needed flexibility to address these underlying causes of hunger. We consider the structure of non-emergency programs as a model for other parts of USAID, and while not a food aid reform issue per se would encourage the committee to look at the nonemergency, multisectoral approach as a successful model for development programs. We would also urge the committee to support this important flexibility and maintain existing authorities for title II nonemergency programs in any future authorizing or reform legislation.

Again, we would like to thank the chairman for holding this important hearing and his continued leadership to improving the U.S. Government's response to food insecurity. We look forward to supporting your, and the committee's, efforts to make every taxpayer dollar as effective as possible in the fight against global hunger.

End Notes

[1] Local and Regional Procurement: a Case Study of Mercy Corps' Programming in Haiti, Kyrgyzstan and Niger.
[2] "Funding Development Projects through the Purchase, Shipment, and Sale of U.S. Commodities Is In efficient and Can Cause Adverse Market Impacts." GAO–11–636. June, 2011.
[3] UNICEF Global Appeal January 2014.

WRITTEN STATEMENT OF GAWAIN KRIPKE, POLICY DIRECTOR, OXFAM AMERICA, WASHINGTON, DC

MOVING FROM FOOD AID TO FLOOD ASSISTANCE: BROADENING THE HORIZONS OF THE FOOD FOR PEACE PROGRAM

Chairman Corker, Senator Cardin, members of the committee, thank you for holding this hearing on the critical need to strengthen a vital program to fight global hunger: international food aid. Oxfam is providing this statement for the record to identify issues and concerns with the current Food for Peace programs and to urge the committee to take steps to increase the impact and improve the overall efficiency and effectiveness of the U.S. food aid program.

Oxfam America is a global organization working to right the wrongs of hunger, poverty, and injustice. As one of 17 members of an international confederation, we work with people in more than 90 countries to create lasting solutions, including saving lives in emergency settings, developing long-term solutions to poverty and campaigning for social change. Our concerns regarding the current Food for Peace program are grounded in more than 60 years of institutional experience working on food emergencies as well as our research and policy analysis on a wide range of agriculture and food security issues, of which food aid is one important aspect. Oxfam America does not take U.S. Government assistance and Oxfam affiliates do not implement U.S. food aid projects.

It is important to acknowledge and applaud the generosity of the American people in serving as the world's most generous donor of food aid. Each year, the United States provides approximately half of all food aid globally. This proud history has helped to reach hundreds of millions of people suffering from acute and chronic hunger, in both emergency and nonemergency settings. The need for this assistance remains as urgent as ever: according to latest estimates, one in nine people around the world are food insecure,[1] and due to current crises in, Iraq and South Sudan among other places, 77.9 million people will need humanitarian assistance, including food, in 2015.[2]

Given this overwhelming need, U.S. assistance must be designed and delivered to maximize reach and impact. Currently, it is not optimized for these purposes. Public Law 480, also known as the Food for Peace Act, has not kept up with best practices in the delivery of food assistance thus undermining the humanitarian focus of this aid program. It was authorized in 1954, and while some amendments have been made to law since then, the fundamental approach to U.S. food aid—buying food from the United States and shipping it overseas, often on U.S.-flag vessels—remains fundamentally unchanged.

Moving from food aid to food assistance

There are and will remain instances where U.S.-procured food aid is necessary, but, this approach is both outdated and inappropriate in many cases. In-kind food aid distributions, of the kind supported through U.S. food aid projects, are most appropriate in instances where food availability is limited in the immediate area; and/or where markets are not effectively functioning. But as is often the case even in the midst of food crises, it is not markets that have collapsed; rather very poor households have no income to purchase available food.

Activities such as local and regional procurement and the use of vouchers or delivery of cash for food security purposes are all proven, effective ways of delivering assistance. For more than a decade, Oxfam and other aid organizations, in collaboration with donors and multilateral agencies, have been experimenting with evaluating and refining the use of these tools to support vulnerable communities facing food insecurity. From early pilot projects in Pakistan and Malawi, to ongoing efforts to meet the needs of refugees affected by the Syria conflict, there is a robust and growing body of evidence documenting the efficacy of taking a more flexible response to food emergencies, one that does not rely primarily or exclusively on purchasing and shipping grain and other food items from the United States.

Building on this body of evidence, the 2008 Farm Bill authorized a Local and Regional Procurement Project. The experience and lessons learned from the Pilot Project were well documented.[3] They showed that, for most commodities, getting locally procured food aid to people in need is cheaper resulting in significant cost savings. Locally procured unprocessed cereals, for example, were 35 percent less expensive on a delivered basis than food aid purchased and shipped from the United States. Additionally, by eliminating the need for transoceanic shipping, LRP projects also resulted in substantial time-savings as well 56 days on average (LRP) compared to 101 days (U.S.-sourced).[4] In a companion study, researchers at Cornell University found that the procurement of food aid on local or regional markets did not induce higher food prices. Additionally, recipients reported being more satisfied with locally purchased food aid since it tended to be a more familiar product.[5]

The Local and Regional Procurement Project became a permanent program in the 2014 Farm Bill. However, this program does not amend the main titles of the Food for Peace Act (title II being the most widely used program under the Food for Peace Act). Moreover, the program did not receive appropriations in 2014, the first year it was available for funding.

In Oxfam's own experience, the use of cash can also meet food security objectives. In 2012 in response to an expected food crisis across the Sahel region—resulting from among other things a drought induced crop failure that threatened to worsen already high levels of chronic food insecurity in the region—Oxfam designed and delivered a cash-based intervention in the Tillabery region of Niger. The project targeted highly vulnerable households, and the distribution schedule coincided with the harvest, giving households the opportunity to stockpile grain at a low price. Followup surveys found that the average recipient household spent more than half the assistance they received on food and that a significant number of these households reported improved food security status. These households were also less likely than the control sample to go into debt for food purchases.[6] Among the uses of the remaining cash not spent on food, households reported investing in livestock and agriculture products and paying school fees. These expenditures represent strategic investments that may make food aid interventions less necessary in the future.

The Food for Peace Act should be updated to allow the U.S. Agency for International Development to utilize a broader set of tools in reaching food insecure households in need of support. Doing so will modernize U.S. assistance, moving from a one-size-fits-all food aid paradigm to a broader, more inclusive food assistance paradigm. Critically, it will improve the overall functionality of the program, increase the number of beneficiaries that can be reached with U.S. taxpayer dollars, and ensure programs are appropriately tailored to specific contexts.

Addressing the agriculture cargo preference requirement

In addition to the Food for Peace Act, the Cargo Preference Act of 1954 also has an important bearing on how U.S.-sourced food aid is delivered. Under current law, at least 50 percent of food aid must be shipped on vessels registered in the United States, with a largely U.S.-citizen mariner crew and flying the U.S. flag. This requirement is intended to ensure the existence of a robust U.S.-flag fleet. It also links humanitarian food aid with national security interests since the purpose of the U.S.-flag vessel requirement is to ensure adequate sealift capacity during times of national emergencies requiring military response. However, the U.S.-flag oceangoing fleet has suffered a significant decline over the last 50 years, a trend that the agriculture cargo preference program has had little impact over.

The agriculture cargo preference (ACP) requirement is both costly and is the subject of political capture. In a review of this program, researchers found that this requirement drives up the cost of shipping. The difference between the lowest competitive bid for shipment and the winning U.S.-flag bid is known as Ocean Freight Differential (OFD). It has been estimated that fulfilling the U.S.-flag vessel requirement has cost U.S. taxpayers $146 million annually in OFD.[7] Moreover, these gains are captured by a small number of companies. Analysis conducted by George Mason University, just three companies—Maersk, Sealift and Liberty—handle 80 percent of food aid shipments.[8]

Given the scarcity of resources and the overwhelming humanitarian need, the Agriculture Cargo Preference requirement should be scrapped, allowing USAID and USDA to use the lowest cost carrier to deliver food aid that requires ocean transportation.

In the absence of the elimination of the agriculture cargo preference requirement, other more immediate reforms can be taken to improve the delivery of U.S. food aid. For instance, in previous years, USAID was reimbursed for OFD charges resulting from the U.S.-flag vessel requirement. This reimbursement was eliminated with the Budget Act of 2013, so food aid administering agencies now bear the full cost of these programs. This reimbursement could be reinstated.

Additionally, changes in how the 50 percent ACP requirement is calculated can reduce costs and improve aid delivery. However, no formal agreement on this issue has been reached between USAID and the Department of Transportation's Maritime Administration (MARAD). One potential explanation for this is MARAD's unwillingness to properly balance the interests of its client companies against those of another agency of the Federal Government. The problems with agriculture cargo preference demonstrate how food aid and the issue of cargo preference are seen by some—both inside Congress and out—as first and foremost a tool to subsidize American industry.

An alternative approach to the issue of cargo preference would be to more fully engage the Department of Defense in its administration and to reimburse food aid implementing agencies for the higher costs of using U.S.-flag vessels.

Ending the practice of monetization

The 1990 Farm Bill included a provision to allow for the sale of U.S.-sourced food aid on developing country markets. Presently, at least 15 percent of nonemergency food aid must be monetized. Aid organizations have used this practice to generate revenue to fund food and nutrition related development activities. These are important projects, but the use of monetization is an inefficient mechanism and at worst risks undermining local markets and negatively impacting small-scale producers.

The Government Accountability Office has looked extensively at the P.L. 480 Food Aid program, including the use of monetization. Their findings document massive waste in monetization activities due to the inability of organizations undertaking monetization to recoup the full cost of purchase and transportation in end market sales. Between 2009 and 2011, the GAO found that $219 million in food aid was lost in the process of monetization.[9] Had USAID and USDA the ability to fund these development activities directly rather than relying on monetization, these savings could have resulted in a greater number of people reached through the U.S. Food for Peace program. It would have additionally avoided any potentially negative market impacts resulting from monetization activities.

In recent years, USAID has taken steps to reduce the use of monetization. Changes in the 2014 Farm Bill increased the percentage of funds that could be used to pay for program costs not related to direct commodity distribution. In addition, USAID has drawn on Development Assistance funds, outside of the of P.L. 480 budget, to augment food aid funding and ensure that development programs do not have to monetize. However, without a specific change in law eliminating the use of monetization, some monetization will occur (at least at the 15 percent minimum) and USAID could return to a substantially greater use of monetization with all of its inherent risks and inefficiencies.

By moving from an in-kind food aid program to a food assistance approach, adapting tools to specific contexts and ensuring a steady and predictable flow of funding for nonemergency food security projects, the use of monetization would not be necessary to fund highly impactful development activities.

Breaking political gridlock to reform the Food for Peace Act

In both the previous and current administrations, proposals have been put forward to reform the Food for Peace Act. At the same time, Congress has sought a path forward that would untie a percentage of U.S. food aid, allowing for it to be used flexibly. In the context of the 2014 Farm Bill, an amendment in the House of Representatives to overhaul U.S. food aid fell just 9 votes short of passage on a strong bipartisan basis. More recently, the Food for Peace Reform Act of 2015, introduced by Senators Corker and Coons proposes a bold transformation of U.S. food aid that addresses the issues and concerns identified in this statement.

The budget proposals by the administration as well as the legislative proposal introduced by Senators Corker and Coons deserve consideration and vote by Congress. The Senate Committee on Foreign Relations has an important role to play in reviewing the P.L. 480 program and in working with the Agriculture Committee, the current committee of jurisdiction for P.L. 480, to develop solid, ambitious reforms that will reinvigorate support for the program, eliminate inefficiencies and ensure continued focus of the program on meeting humanitarian and development objectives.

End Notes

[1] U.N. Food and Agriculture Organization (2014)" State of Food Insecurity in the World: Strengthening the Enabling Environment for Food Security and Nutrition."
[2] UNOCHA (2015) "Global Humanitarian Overview: 2015."
[3] See: US Department of Agriculture (2012) "USDA Local and Regional Procurement Pilot Project: Independent Evaluation Report."
[4] Ibid.
[5] Lentz, et. al. (2012) "The Impacts of Local and Regional Procurement of U.S. Food Aid: Learning Alliance Synthesis Report."
[6] Tumusiime, E (2015) "Do Early Cash Transfers in a Food Crisis Improve Resilience? Evidence from Niger." Development in Practice 25:2, 174–187.
[7] Barrett, C. (2010) "Food Aid and Agriculture Cargo Preference." Note that this is for fiscal year 2006 only.
[8] Ferris, W. (2014) "Impact of US Government Food Aid Reforms on the U.S. Shipping Industry: Preliminary Results."
[9] U.S. Government Accountability Office (2010) "International Food Assistance: Funding Development Projects Through the Purchase, Shipment and Sale of U.S. Commodities is Inefficient and can Cause Adverse Market Impacts."

WRITTEN STATEMENT OF SAVE THE CHILDREN

On behalf of Save the Children, we thank Chairman Bob Corker, former Ranking Member Bob Menendez and members of this committee for holding this hearing and for the opportunity to submit written testimony. Save the Children strongly supports the need to pursue common-sense reforms of U.S. international food aid that will benefit millions of vulnerable children and families in need around the world.

Save the Children invests in childhood—every day, in times of crisis and for our future. We are in our 83rd year as a child-focused, nonprofit organization working to inspire breakthroughs in the way the world treats children and to achieve immediate and lasting change in their lives. Today we work in 21 states across the nation and 120 countries in the developing world to give children a healthy start, the opportunity to learn and protection from harm. In 2013, our programs helped more than 143 million children worldwide, including 250,000 in the United States.

Save the Children has been designing and implementing some of the most complex international food security and nutrition programs for more than five decades. In addition to building long-term resilience to reduce chronic hunger for children and their families, we also mobilize rapid life-saving assistance for people caught in humanitarian emergencies such as Syria, Iraq, South Sudan, and Yemen.

Our organization is a proud partner and implementer of Food for Peace emergency and nonemergency programs. Currently, Save the Children is implementing Food For Peace programs in 13 countries totaling around $350 million. In addition, Save the Children is the second-largest implementer for the U.N. World Food Programme (WFP)—the largest recipient of Food For Peace P.L. 480 Title II emergency funding. In 2013, Save the Children distributed 125,000 Metric Tons of emergency food commodities for WFP, reaching an estimated 1 million people. We stand by the food security work we do with Food For Peace in saving and transforming children's lives.

As cochair of the Modernizing Foreign Effectiveness Network (MFAN), Save the Children is strongly committed to aid effectiveness and the goal to maximize efficiencies in U.S. policy by eliminating wasteful rules and regulations. In alignment with our leadership in MFAN, and based on our organization's own experience on the ground, we support food aid reforms that will make a concrete difference for children globally. We urge Congress and the administration to make P.L. 480 Title II food aid (also referred to as U.S. food assistance) more efficient and cost effective in order to allow U.S. food assistance programs to reach more children at no additional cost.

CRITICAL IMPORTANCE OF U.S. FOOD ASSISTANCE

Great progress has been made in the fight against hunger and malnutrition. In just the last decade, the world has witnessed a dramatic and positive shift for children. Extreme poverty has been cut in half; 100 million people have escaped from hunger; and the numbers of children dying under the age of 5 fell at a faster rate than ever before. Investments in United States Agency for International Development (USAID) and specifically the Food For Peace program have made a vital contribution to these gains and are directly helping to reduce global food and nutrition insecurity and achieve the U.S. global commitment to ending preventable child deaths.

Despite this progress however, hunger and malnutrition still remain unacceptably high. One in every eight people around the world faces chronic hunger and an estimated 100 million people endure extreme hunger crises. In sub-Saharan Africa the numbers are even higher, with one in four people undernourished. Malnutrition is the underlying cause of nearly half (3.1 million) of all child deaths under 5 and can reduce a country's Gross Domestic Product by as much as 16.5 percent (UNECA, The Cost of Hunger in Africa, 2014). Chronic child malnutrition remains stubbornly high, causing 165 million children to suffer stunted physical and cognitive growth that robs them of reaching their full potential. Experts estimate the return on investment in nutrition to be $16 for every $1 dollar invested—a ratio comparable to infrastructure (Global Nutrition Report, 2014). Experts also show that investments in agricultural growth is at least two times as effective at reducing poverty as growth in other sectors (World Bank, 2008).

During the 2007 global food price crisis that pushed an estimated 100 million additional people into poverty, some 60 food riots and protests raged in nations across the globe. Scholars and others point to the fundamental food crisis as a key trigger of the political upheavals of the Arab Spring. U.S. investments to combat global food and nutrition insecurity are invaluable. The benefit of such investments are inextricably linked to the security of our Nation and creating a more stable and prosperous world.

While Save the Children supports U.S. food aid reform, we also strongly support robust funding of the Food For Peace P.L. 480 Title II program (also referred to as the Food For Peace program). Food For Peace is the primary vehicle providing U.S. emergency food aid and multiyear food security development to millions of children and families each year. In 2013, Food for Peace title II made an enormous difference in the lives of almost 36 million people experiencing deep, acute or chronic poverty and food insecurity. The Office's unique focus on serving the poorest, most vulnerable, most chronically food insecure people acts as a foundation for other development investments. It also has the greatest level of expertise in implementing interdisciplinary, integrated approaches to tackle the most complex development problems. These multisectoral programs play a vital role in addressing child malnutrition, preventing famines and building the resilience of vulnerable populations to withstand future shocks. Robust investments in Food For Peace not only helps the United States address current crises but also helps prevent future emergencies as well.

SUPPORT FOR FOOD AID REFORM

While the United States remains the largest donor of global food assistance, there has been a sharp net drop of over half a billion dollars in title II funding since 2009. Transportation costs of U.S. food aid have also risen dramatically. We urge Congress to increase funding of Food For Peace P.L. 480 Title II in fiscal year 2016 to $1.75 billion from its current $1.466 billion. At the same time, we also recognize that tight budget constraints and continued global demand for food assistance make it more important than ever that U.S. taxpayer dollars be spent in the most efficient way possible to maximize reach and effectiveness.

Save the Children has been a long-time supporter of both U.S. international food aid and food aid reform. To our organization, reforming U.S. food aid is about making an excellent program even better by increasing its reach and cost-effectiveness. The inefficiencies of U.S. food aid stem from the rules of the P.L. 480 Title II account that tie U.S. food assistance almost entirely to American-grown agricultural commodities and strict cargo preference requirements. The inefficiencies of these rules are well documented by the General Accountability Office and teams of independent academic researchers led by Christopher Barrett at Cornell University. They are further complemented by published results of the U.S. Department of Agriculture's (USDA) Pilot Local and Regional Procurement program authorized in the 2008 Farm Bill.

Large portions of U.S. international food aid are inefficiently spent on shipping and handling rather than used to reach more children. In 2012, almost 50 cents of every $1 of U.S. was spent on shipping and handling. (For example, in 2012 ocean freight and inland transport costs were 58 percent for emergency and 37 percent for nonemergency, totaling 47.5 percent.) We are encouraged by the momentum in Congress and the administration to address this issue. Our organization has been supportive of a variety of thoughtful and constructive reform proposals. These include the President's proposed reforms in his budget requests starting in fiscal year 2014 as well as the reform amendment introduced by House Foreign Affairs Chair and Ranking Members, Representatives Royce and Engel, which lost by just nine votes in the House of Representatives vote on the 2014 Farm Bill. It also includes the immensely helpful incremental reforms that passed in the 2014 Farm Bill and 2014 Omnibus and the expansive reform proposal put forth by Senators Bob Corker and Chris Coons in the Food For Peace Reform Act (S. 525).

All of these reform proposals mentioned above have had at least three key elements in common that elicited Save the Children's support.

1. *Food aid reforms would result in reaching more children—sometimes millions more, using the same level of investment.* In the case of the Royce-Engel amendment for example, which increased the flexibility of title II to 45 percent and kept 55 percent of food aid tied to U.S. agricultural commodities, the reach of the program would have increased by 2 to 4 million more people. The recent Corker-Coons proposal, which completely unties U.S. food aid from U.S. agriculture and cargo preference requirements, is estimated to increase the reach of title II by as many as 12 million more people. The estimates all include varying assumptions that range in uncertainty, including annual levels of funding, but even the most conservative estimates would dramatically increase the numbers of children reached.

2. *Reforms would result in a reduced need to monetize food commodities, the practice of reselling U.S. food commodities in local and regional markets to raise funds for USAID title II development programs.* USAID and the General Accountability Office (GAO) estimate losses from monetization to be 25 to 30 percent on average (GAO–11–636 and USAID Behind the Numbers). The Agriculture Act of 2014 (2014 Farm Bill) made great progress in this area by increasing the percentage of cash-based resources allowed to be used as part of title II from 7 percent to 20 percent. It also expanded the types of expenses the cash can be used to cover. These changes, together with an additional $35 million of title II funds made flexible by The Con-

solidated Appropriations Act of 2014, combined to allow USAID to stop monetizing commodities, except to meet the mandatory minimum of 15 percent monetization that still remains in law.

3. *Reforms would increase the level of flexibility USAID has to use the most appropriate tool in the toolbox to respond to crises quickly and effectively. These tools include cash transfers, food vouchers, local and regional purchase of food (LRP), as well as in-kind food commodities.* Improving the United States ability to respond to humanitarian emergencies and chronic food and nutrition insecurity with all tools in the toolbox would help ensure the most appropriate response for any given context based on a needs assessment and market analysis. The incremental increases of flexibility in the 2014 Farm Bill were very helpful but were insufficient to allow USAID to both reduce the need to monetize commodities in development projects and to respond more rapidly and most appropriately to humanitarian emergencies.

If time is of the essence, which it commonly is in emergencies, then buying food closer to where it is needed can save time and reduce costs. The U.S. Department of Labor's pilot study on local and regional procurement of food aid authorized in the 2008 Farm Bill found local purchase of food to be 74 days, or over 2 months, faster than shipping in-kind commodities from the United States (USDA Local and Regional Food Aid Procurement Pilot Project Independent Evaluation Report, December 2012). Other studies also reported LRP to be 25 percent less expensive than delivering in-kind commodities and recipients to be more satisfied with the locally purchased food they received (Learning Alliance Synthesis Report, 2012). USAID finds that cash transfers and food vouchers overall also save time and costs. As an implementer of U.S. emergency and nonemergency food aid, Save the Children has found that leveraging local markets can create durable solutions. By incentivizing local farmers and working through the market to provide goods and services, people are invested, opportunities avail themselves, economic resilience is built and lives improve.

In-kind food commodities still play a critical role in U.S. food aid, particularly in areas of acute food crises where markets have failed. However, increasing the flexibility to use all response tools will reduce risks, mitigate unintended consequences and help ensure the most appropriate response to the type of crisis. The risks were summed up in a recent report on U.S. Food Aid Programs released this month by the Congressional Research Service, ''U.S. reliance on in-kind food aid has become controversial for several reasons: it is slower and more costly than cash transfers; it tends to cause commodity price distortions and volatility in local markets where monetization . . . occurs; it can impede commercial exports; and it has engendered international concerns from key trade partners who contend that it is a form of export subsidy and potentially conflicts with the intent of international trade agreements.''

UNLOCKING INNOVATION AND EFFICIENCY: E–TRANSFER CASH PROGRAMMING

The food aid reforms passed in the 5-year 2014 Farm Bill provided over $103 million per year in additional flexibility to use cash-based programming where appropriate. That increase is helping to drive new innovations in delivering cash-programming via digital transactions using various electronic platforms. Further increases to make title II more flexible would not only be transformational in the lives of the poor but also in the way development programs are delivered in the 21st century.

Cash-based programming supports the needs of communities in crisis through various means. These include food vouchers as well as multiple forms of conditional and unconditional cash transfers, such as cash for work or training programs. Cash-based programming has been an effective and cost-efficient part of food and nutrition security programming for several years. A recent 2015 GAO report affirmed this view by finding that cash-based programming is an effective tool to deliver U.S. food assistance and that this modality is an established and proven practice in the international donor community (GAO–15–328).

Cash and vouchers are particularly useful in areas where it is too dangerous, difficult, or costly to provide in-kind food commodities, such as areas in conflict or that are too remote or inaccessible. Save the Children also finds cash and vouchers to be strong delivery modalities in areas where food markets are strong and where U.S. assistance can strengthen the livelihoods and resilience of local small-scale producers to withstand future shocks or stresses. Perhaps most importantly, cash transfers provided to female participants are known to empower women by increasing their ability to partake in household decisions, mobilize resources, and have agency over various aspects of their lives (IFPRI, Women's Empowerment Evidence Review, 2013). Evidence has long shown that increasing women's agency and empowerment is critical to improving nutrition outcomes for their children and themselves.

Due to technological developments around the world and changes in connectivity, cash-based programming is currently in the midst of a rapid revolution through the use of digital transactions in place of paper. This new electronic approach could be transformational for people's lives by expanding the number of platforms through which financial services can be delivered to the poor and unbanked. It is widely recognized that the cost barriers are too high for regular brick and mortar banking companies to profitably provide financial services to those at the base of the economic pyramid. Yet, increasing access to financial services has long been identified as a key pathway out of poverty by helping people expand their options, better manage risks, create safety nets, and improve their health and education.

The mobile banking program in Kenya, M–PESA, is well known for expanding the use of the mobile phone as a new platform to deliver financial services including payments, transfers, insurance, savings, and credit. Indeed, of the estimated 2.5 billion people in the world that are unbanked and lack financial services to support their livelihoods or protect their assets, more than 1 billion have access to a mobile phone (Mobile Money for the Unbanked Programme, State of the Industry, 2013). This is a statistic not lost on mobile phone companies expanding operations in the developing world. But digital transactions platforms can come in many forms, not just through phones. Digital transfers are also being done through transactions companies via plastic cards. Today, Save the Children is developing new, innovative approaches for cash-based programming through both mobile banking and electronic transfers, the benefits of which are likely to be transformational to people's lives and livelihoods.

For example, Save the Children is currently in partnership with the global technology and transactions company, MasterCard, to develop new, innovative ways to deliver digital cash-based programs aimed at improving food and nutrition security and strengthening the resilience of people in Yemen. It is worthwhile to note that the partnership is carried out between Save the Children and MasterCard's products development department, as opposed to its philanthropy arm. The program with MasterCard will reach approximately 9,000 households in three districts over 3 years. It will focus on providing cash vouchers that provide food in exchange for work rebuilding community assets such as water canals, harvesting structures, terraces and roads. The rest of the project focuses on improved infant and young child feeding practices through participation in community-based groups, awareness campaigns and skills training.

The traditional paper vouchers are time-intensive to distribute, collect, and reconcile. The electronic voucher system saves time for program participants to engage in livelihood activities, attend trainings or provide family care instead of traveling to, and from, central locations to collect monthly vouchers. To get the food, participants go to any one of the many participating vendors and use their electronic card and pin number. Small-scale vendors who redeem the vouchers also save time and improve the accuracy of their records by tracking payments electronically. As both the vendors and the participants are become more accustomed to using electronic transactions, it can open the way to using other electronic financial services. Lastly, development practitioners save time by not having to collect and reconcile the paperwork and instead are able to spend that time on monitoring, impact analysis, and quality assurance. Use of the new technology will also make strides in learning by having a detailed track record of participants' transactions that made available through MasterCard's global data repository.

SUPPORT FOR FOOD FOR PEACE PROGRAM

U.S. food assistance programs under P.L. 480 Title II have served as a foundation of global efforts to confront the challenge of global hunger and malnutrition. The Food For Peace program maintains both emergency programs that keep people alive, and developmental food security programs that address the underlying sources of chronic hunger and malnutrition.

To this day, the title II Food For Peace program remains the main program in the U.S. Government laser-focused on creating pathways out of poverty for the poorest, most vulnerable, most chronically food insecure people. When provided at the right time, economic or food assistance gives households the means to endure hard times while remaining on a pathway out of poverty. It helps families avoid difficult and consequential choices between eating a meal or selling their most important asset, sending a child to school or going to the doctor. The Food For Peace program is skilled at doing complex food and nutrition security programming with multisectoral, interdisciplinary approaches to get at immediate impacts and root causes. The experts at Food For Peace have long recognized that addressing child malnutrition is essential to breaking the cycle of poverty and hunger. As such the program ensures that children get the right food at the right time, particularly during the 1,000 day window between pregnancy and a child's second birthday.

Through partnering with Food For Peace, Save the Children has built a base of innovations in food production and consumption, water and sanitation, social behavioral change, and local partnerships. The lessons learned from our projects are shared through the Food For Peace-funded Technical and Operational Performance Support (TOPS) program, an open community of implementers sharing best practices in food security and nutrition programming—all leading to greater results in food and nutrition security.

For these reasons, Save the Children is dedicated to working with Congress to support and maintain investments in U.S. food assistance. In fiscal year 2016, we urge Congress to bring funding of the P.L. 480 Title II program up to at least to $1.75 billion in fiscal year 2016, which still represents a decline from previous years. At the same time, we look forward to working with Congress and the administration to find a pathway forward that maintains the strong level of support title II currently enjoys and achieves reforms that increase the numbers of children reached and the speed and flexibility of the program to appropriately respond to disasters and crises around the world.

ANNEX 1

In April 2013, Save the Children worked with CARE USA, Catholic Relief Services, Mercy Corps, and World Vision to draft a set of principles around food aid reform that still hold firm today. These principles were also endorsed by the following organizations: InterAction, Alliance for Global Food Security, Concern Worldwide US, Helen Keller International, International Relief & Development, International Rescue Committee, Land O'Lakes International Development, Lutheran World Relief, Mercy-USA for Aid and Development, Partners for Development, Relief International, World Food Program USA, World Renew.

Principle #1: Reforms should protect the core focus and effective elements of existing food assistance programs. U.S. food assistance programs are unique in their focus on hunger and malnutrition among the poorest and most vulnerable populations. Emergency programs respond to urgent needs while developmental programs strengthen the resiliency of people facing chronic food insecurity, and employ a community-based multisector approach that addresses agricultural productivity, nutrition, and livelihoods. These programs provide a stable multiyear commitment of support that is critical to achieving lasting results. Reforms should not alter or undermine these important elements of the current system.

Principle #2: Reforms should increase the number of people helped. In 2012, U.S. food assistance reached 46 million people. Yet since 2000 the amount of U.S. food assistance has declined by more than half, primarily due to decreases in funding and higher commodity, transportation, and distribution costs. Reforms should seek to offset this decline by increasing the number of people served in both emergency and developmental food assistance programs, and should not be used simply to justify funding cuts. Every effort should be made to reinvest savings achieved through reform into both programs.

Principle #3: Reforms should increase the flexibility of food assistance programs. Allowing significantly more flexible use of tools such as cash transfers, food vouchers, and local and regional procurement, alongside provision of U.S. commodities and direct program funding, would provide a variety of program and resource options to help ensure the most appropriate response in each context. Such flexibility would improve program efficiency and impact and increase the number of people reached.

Principle #4: Reforms to food assistance programs should be made in an open, transparent, and inclusive process. As both implementers and advocates, the nonprofit and civil society communities are major partners and supporters of food assistance programs. We bring important perspectives on how to maximize program effectiveness and reach, as well as wide grassroots networks that provide public support for these programs. Civil society engagement is crucial to the effectiveness and political viability of the reform process and to the future success of these programs in meeting the needs of poor people.

WRITTEN STATEMENT OF DR. CAROLYN WOO, PRESIDENT AND CHIEF EXECUTIVE
OFFICER OF CATHOLIC RELIEF SERVICES

Thank you Chairman Corker and Ranking Member Cardin for receiving this testimony on behalf of Catholic Relief Services (CRS) and for holding this hearing examining ways in which food aid programs can be improved.

Catholic Relief Services is the international relief and development agency of the U.S. Conference of Catholic Bishops. Our work reaches millions of poor and vulnerable people in nearly 90 countries. CRS works with people and communities based on need, without regard to race, creed, or nationality. CRS often partners with institutions of the Catholic Church and other local civil society groups in the implementation of programs, which from our experience is essential to understanding the needs of the communities we work with, and ultimately the long-term success of our work.

Catholic Relief Services is one of the largest implementers of international food aid programs, including the Food for Peace program. CRS implements both emergency and nonemergency development programs through Food for Peace. We offer this testimony from the perspective of an implementer.

FOOD AID REFORM EFFORTS

For many years, Catholic Relief Services has been one of the leading voices for reforms to U.S. international food aid. Today, our main reform objectives are, to the extent possible: (1) minimize and eliminate if possible the need to monetize food aid resources; (2) minimize the impacts that cargo preference laws have on food aid programs; and (3) maximize the discretion that implementers have in choosing whether to use U.S. commodities, locally produced/purchased commodities, vouchers, or cash transfers in the implementation of programs. We actively championed these kinds of reforms in both the 2008 and 2014 Farm Bills and for several years in the annual appropriations process.

Over this time, we believe there have been incremental but important improvements to the food aid system. Thanks to the work of the Agriculture Committees and Appropriators, we have seen changes in the recent Farm Bill and in recent Agriculture Appropriations bills that allowed for the reduction of monetization in Food for Peace programming. In the Farm Bill we also saw the establishment of a permanent Local and Regional Procurement (LRP) program under the auspices of the U.S. Department of Agriculture. We have also seen a steady increase in funding for the Emergency Food Security Program (EFSP) that provides resources for local purchase, vouchers, and cash transfers during emergencies, which the administration has championed and State and Foreign Operations Appropriators have supported.

In addition to these efforts, we think more can be done to reform how the food aid system works in the areas of monetization, cargo preference, and discretion in the tools used in programs.

MONETIZATION

As noted earlier, Catholic Relief Services seeks to minimize, and eliminate if possible, the need to monetize food aid resources. Monetization is the process of shipping U.S. commodities overseas, to be sold abroad to raise funds to cover nonfood program costs. Usually the markets in which these goods must be sold cannot bear the full cost of purchasing U.S. commodities and delivering them there, thus most sales are at a loss. The Government Accountability Office has looked at this and has concluded that monetization is an inefficient means of raising funds to cover nonfood program costs, noting that Food for Peace monetization on average achieved 76 percent cost recovery—that is, the sale of commodities netted only 76 percent of the cost to buy and transport the food in the first place.[1] Our own experience closely resembles these results.

Catholic Relief Services acknowledges that substantial progress toward reducing monetization within Food for Peace was made in the 2014 Farm Bill, and thanks to these reforms CRS is not monetizing in any of the Food for Peace programs we are currently implementing. However, we note that the Farm Bill maintained a requirement that at least 15 percent of Food for Peace development program resources have to be used toward monetization. This enduring 15 percent requirement could force our programs in the future to monetize again. We ask Congress to consider measures that would eliminate the requirement to monetize in Food for Peace programs altogether. We also ask Congress to provide additional direct funding to development programs sufficient to cover program expenses so that monetization need not be used in these programs.

CARGO PREFERENCE

Catholic Relief Services also seeks to minimize the impact that cargo preference laws have on food aid programs. Cargo preference is the policy that requires the shipping of U.S. impelled cargo, in this case food aid, on U.S.-flagged vessels. The basis for this requirement is to help maintain private, sealift capacity—in terms of both cargo vessels and U.S. crews—in order to transport military supplies should it be required. While there is debate over whether cargo preference is an effective way of achieving this objective, we can tell you that as an implementer of food aid programs that the cargo preference law, and the ways in which the law has been applied to food aid, leads to higher than necessary transportation costs for food aid programs, reducing the amount of food commodities that can be bought and thus the number of people served by food aid programs.

The reason that the mandatory use of U.S.-flagged cargo vessels to deliver food aid drives up transportation costs is that U.S.-flagged vessels are substantially more expensive than other available vessels. According to a study commissioned by the Maritime Administration, U.S.-flagged vessels cost 2.7 times more to operate than vessels flagged in other countries.[2] Our own experience in the price differential between U.S. and other vessels matches well this assessment. As such, we would prefer that cargo preference laws not apply to any of the food aid programs—Food for Peace, Food for Education, or Food for Progress. If this is not possible, we ask that Congress consider making changes in how cargo preference laws are applied that will reduce the burden placed on budgets of these food aid programs, close loopholes that allow U.S. carriers to manipulate regulations for their economic benefit, and improve transparency.

Current cargo preference law applicable to food aid programs is found in 46 USC 55305(b), and states that: "at least 50 percent of the gross tonnage of the . . . commodities (computed separately for dry bulk carriers, dry cargo liners, and tankers) which may be transported on ocean vessels is transported on privately-owned commercial vessels of the United States, to the extent those vessels are available at fair and reasonable rates for commercial vessels of the United States, in a manner that will ensure a fair and reasonable participation of commercial vessels of the United States in those cargoes by geographic areas."

We posit that current applications of this law also drive up costs needlessly. For instance, the Maritime Administration, supported by the Department of Justice, has determined "that at least [50] percent of agricultural commodities be shipped by U.S. flag vessels 'computed separately for dry bulk carriers, dry cargo liners and tankers' requires that the U.S. vessels be divided into those three categories and further, that the [50] percent minimum be computed separately for each category of vessel."[3] We have seen U.S. carriers use this provision to force the rebidding of awards that were initially to less expensive carriers (both U.S. and foreign) because the quota for the vessel type they were offering had not been met. Additionally, the reference to "geographic areas" has led to the requirement that food aid programs meet the 50 percent quota by country.[4] Under this constraint, large programs that require multiple shipments in a year can potentially make use of less expensive foreign flag carriers for some of their commodity deliveries, but small country programs with only one or two shipments in a year likely will have to use the more expensive U.S. carriers for all their commodities in order to ensure they meet the 50 percent minimum.

While we are champions of reforming how cargo preference law is applied to food aid programs, we also recognize that U.S. merchant mariners have been valuable partners in the fight against world hunger since the inception of the Food for Peace program 60 years ago. Their efforts and sacrifices in the delivery of U.S. food have helped to save and improve countless lives around the globe. As an organization, Catholic Relief Services has great respect and admiration for the men and women who are part of the U.S. merchant marine and we would be glad to have them continue their role in the fight against hunger. However, we believe that achieving the objective of maintaining a U.S.-flagged merchant fleet, and U.S. mariners to crew those vessels, should not come at the expense of more efficient food aid programs. We encourage Congress to consider measures to support merchant marines in ways that do not place an undue burden on food aid funding but do allow for their continued participation in the delivery of U.S. food aid.

Additionally, we note that at one time the Maritime Administration published data concerning the tonnage of cargo that was shipped by type of carrier (U.S./foreign flagged), per country. This provided a clear, aggregate and public picture of the result of cargo preference requirements. This data has not been published in several years and we suggest that Congress consider requiring such reporting.

IMPLEMENTATION TOOL DISCRETION

In order to respond to varying local contexts, Catholic Relief Services urges Congress to provide implementers as much discretion as possible in whether they use U.S. commodities, locally produced/purchased commodities, vouchers, or cash transfers in their programs. CRS has had experience using all these modes of assistance—U.S. commodities in current food aid programs, and the various Local and Regional Procurement (LRP) modalities in ESFP programs and in the LRP pilot program authorized in the 2008 Farm Bill. From this experience, CRS believes that all these modalities of assistance can be valuable tools in the fight against hunger, but which is the right tool depends greatly on specific circumstances we cannot necessarily know in advance. As such, providing implementers discretion will allow us to evaluate the situation and utilize the most appropriate tool.

Following the implementation of LRP pilot program, Catholic Relief Services and several other implementing organizations worked with Cornell University to evaluate the impacts of their LRP programs.[5] That study found that on average locally procured food, vouchers, and cash resulted in a time savings of nearly 14 weeks compared with shipping food from the United States. It also found cost savings in the local purchase of unprocessed grains and some pulses, but that U.S.-sourced processed foods and vegetable oils were less expensive than local sources. Our understanding from this study, and continued experience with each modality tells us that there are several factors to consider in determining which mode of assistance is best suited for a particular program. These factors include current market prices of the various applicable commodities both in the United States and in the country and region in which the program takes place, cost of overseas transportation, distance from the coast and overall cost of in-land transportation, availability of local food in the necessary quantity and quality, the familiarity the target population has of the type of food being made available, the ability to physically reach the target population, and a host of other considerations.

Because of the many variables to consider it is difficult, if not impossible, to say what the best mode of assistance is, nor can we confidently predict how many more people will be served using one option over another, without knowing the specific conditions in which the food aid response will operate. What we can say is that in some cases using U.S. commodities will be the best choice—because it's less expensive, it can be provided in the necessary quality or quantities, and/or buying locally will negatively impact local markets. Alternatively, in some cases using an LRP modality will be the best choice—because it's less expensive, can get to the target population faster, is more amenable to local diets, and/or because bringing in U.S. commodities would be disruptive to the local market. It should also be noted that what is the best option at a particular point in time may not necessarily be the best option at a later point in time because one or more of the factors listed above has changed.

Given the dynamic circumstances in which food aid operates, food aid programs should be responsive, nimble, and adaptable to current conditions. Ideally, implementers would have complete discretion in how food aid funding is used through the life of a program. Alternatively, we recommend Congress consider making more resources available for LRP purposes, whether through increased funding of EFSP or through changes in Food for Peace that would allow for LRP modalities to be used, and that they be available for programming alongside U.S. commodities through the life of projects.

THE SUCCESS OF FOOD AID PROGRAMS

This hearing is focused on ways in which food aid programs can be made better, but it is important to keep in context that food aid programs are currently highly successful, and this is especially true of the Food for Peace program. As an implementer of both emergency and development Food for Peace programs, we know firsthand how lives are touched and saved by these programs. In your efforts to make these programs better, we urge Congress to also preserve what makes them so successful.

Generally, Food for Peace emergency programs provide victims of civil conflict or natural disasters food rations to help get them through the difficult times they face. While these programs are typically designed to provide 6–12 months of response, in some cases the emergency conditions are protracted indefinitely, as we are seeing in the case of the Syrian refugee crises. The success of emergency programs can be measured in the people who are fed, who wouldn't otherwise have anything to eat. This is achieved through generous funding by Congress—in recent appropriations cycles, over $1 billion has been provided annually for emergency Food for Peace programs.

Food for Peace development programs also provide food to vulnerable groups who might otherwise go hungry, but their primary focus is building the capacity of beneficiaries to feed themselves. Development projects cover a number of sectors—agriculture, nutrition, land regeneration, water management, infrastructure improvements, and market engagement—in order to put whole communities on a sustainable path toward self-reliance. These are multiyear projects that give implementers enough time to achieve real results, like revitalizing a watershed or making a lasting impact on farmers' skill sets. Development programs are awarded on a competitive basis, allowing the best ideas and most successful implementers to carry out the work. And funding for development programs cannot be redirected to other purposes, giving beneficiaries the assurance that they will not be abandoned midstream after the U.S. commitment is made to help them. The success of these programs can be measured in the number of poor farmers who realize the dignity of being able to provide for their families and the ability of communities to withstand droughts and other disasters on their own, without having to rely on emergency food aid to get them through the challenges they face.

By these measures, we can say Food for Peace development programs CRS has implemented have been highly successful. For instance, Ethiopia's Productive Safety Net Program (PSNP), supported in part by a development Food for Peace program, has helped small-farm families weather the 2011 drought that hit the Horn of Africa, prompting Tom Stall, USAID's Ethiopia Mission Director at the time to say "you had a drought that's as big as any in the last 20, 30 years—maybe bigger in terms of Ethiopia—and yet there was no famine. So we've broken that cycle."[6] In Burkina Faso, on a visit to rural farmers 2 years after a CRS-led development program had ended, then-USAID Assistant Administrator Nancy Lindborg noted that "farmers are continuing to thrive on the proceeds of their dry season market gardens."[7] And the FY 2013 International Food Assistance Report reported that as a result of the CRS-led development program in Malawi "farmers in program areas grew enough on their land to be able to sell pigeon peas . . . for use in WFP's emergency response in other districts of the country."[8]

Given the success that emergency and development Food for Peace programs have had, we urge Congress to evaluate any reform proposals not only by the ways they change Food for Peace, but also by the ways in which they preserve those elements of Food for Peace that currently work. These include the focus Food for Peace has had on prioritizing assistance to the poorest and most vulnerable, the continuous learning and sharing of best practices that Food for Peace encourages, the broad political support that has maintained strong levels of funding for the program over the years, and the dedicated, uninterrupted funding that multiyear development programs need to save lives, move people out of poverty, and reduce long-run emergency food assistance needs.

CONCLUSION

Catholic Relief Services has been, and will continue to be a strong supporter of reforms to the U.S. international food aid system. As a Catholic organization, we are guided by Catholic Social Teaching that calls us all to be good stewards of our resources and we believe the changes we outlined above will improve how existing food aid resources are used. Catholic Social Teaching also calls us to protect and promote human life and dignity, by providing those in need with food in emergency programs and by helping the poor and vulnerable break the cycle of poverty and dependence through development programs. Catholic Relief Services believes that any changes to food aid in the name of reform must also preserve those elements of food aid that are effective, or we risk undermining the great work already being done by these programs.

End Notes

[1] Government Accountability Office, "Funding Development Projects through the Purchase, Shipment, and Sale of U.S. Commodities Is Inefficient and Can Cause Adverse Market Impacts," June 2012.

[2] Maritime Administration, U.S. Dept. of Trans., "Comparison of U.S. and Foreign-Flag Operating Costs," Sept. 2011.

[3] Maritime Administration, U.S. Dept. of Trans. "Notice: Procedures for Determining Vessel Service Categories for Purposes of the Cargo Preference Act," Fed. Reg. Vol. 74, No. 177, Sept. 15, 2009 , p. 47309.

[4] Government Accountability Office, "Cargo Preference Requirements: Objectives Not Significantly Advanced When Used in U.S. Food Aid Programs," Sept. 1994.

[5] Erin C. Lentz, Christopher B. Barrett and Miguel I. Gómez, "The Impacts of Local and Regional Procurement of U.S. Food Aid: Learning Alliance Synthesis Report," Final Report: A Multidimensional Analysis of Local and Regional Procurement of U.S. Food Aid, January 2012.

67

[6] Kelly Ramundo, "Catching Ethiopians Before They Fall," USAID Frontlines, May/June 2012.
[7] Nancy Lindborg, "Responding Early and Building Resilience in the Sahel," Huffington Post, Mar. 3, 2012.
[8] USDA/USAID International Food Assistance Report, Fiscal Year 2013.

————

RESPONSES OF DR. VINCENT SMITH TO QUESTIONS
SUBMITTED BY SENATOR DAVID PERDUE

Question. Coming to the Senate from the business sector, I appreciate your recommendations for increasing the efficiency of U.S. food aid to get more out of U.S. taxpayer dollars. I have heard from other sectors that these reforms might impact their industry.

Could you please speak to the impact of food aid reforms on the following sectors:

◆ U.S. agriculture?

Answer. Any effects on the U.S. agriculture sector of the proposed reform are likely to be positive but miniscule. The major bulk commodities provided as food aid, such as wheat and corn, are traded on global markets. Shifting to local and regional sourcing (as well as abandoning cargo preference for food aid and the practice of monetization) will increase the amount of funds available for purchasing all food aid, including those commodities, with a positive effect on global prices and, therefore, prices on local U.S. markets that are clearly and unambiguously linked to the world markets for those commodities.

For processed food aid commodities such as cooking oil and peanut butter, complete flexibility in sourcing will still lead USAID and USDA to source those commodities from the United States as, for these commodities, currently and the near- and medium-term future, the United States is almost certain to remain the low cost and most economically efficient food aid source. Some small acre commodities such as peas and lentils are also sometimes purchased for food aid. Very recent research by Dr. Joseph Janzen at Montana State University finds that food aid purchases of peas and lentils have no measurable impacts on the prices at which those commodities are traded in local U.S. markets as these are also globally traded commodities).

◆ U.S. jobs in our ports?

Answer. A recent George Mason University study estimated that shifting from mandatory sourcing in the United States for food aid would result in the loss of about 175 jobs at U.S. ports if that was all that was happening in those ports. However, they correctly point out that product handling in those ports is growing at a rapid annual rate because of the relatively rapid growth of trade in the U.S. economy (both in terms of exports and imports). The increase in demand for port workers (of all types) because of the expansion of total trade will require many more workers than the jobs that would otherwise by lost because of ending cargo preference for food aid. Thus no actual person is likely to be laid off because of a shift to local sourcing for food aid.

◆ U.S. national security?

Answer. The independent studies (ones not sponsored by the Maritime lobby) and various GAO reports that have examined this issue have concluded that ending cargo preference will have minimal if any substantive effects on the military preparedness of the United States with respect to sealift capacity. The data show that about 70 percent of the privately owned U.S.-flagged vessels used for food aid shipments do not meet the Department of Defense criteria for vessels from the privately owned maritime fleet that can be used for sealift (because they are too old and/or are bulk carriers or tankers unsuited for almost all sealift purposes without major refits). It would be much cheaper for the U.S. Government to directly subsidize only those vessels that meet DOD criteria rather than subsidize food aid shipments carried on vessels that have no military value. The vessels that have no value for the purposes of national security carry the majority of food aid and are retained in service by private mercantile interests (and 40 percent of which are, in the end, foreign owned through U.S.-registered holding companies) because of the high shipping rates that can be charged to the U.S. Government on food aid cargo preference shipments.

◆ U.S. shipping?

Answer. There will be very little effect on U.S. shipping. The DOD estimate is that if cargo preference for food aid were ended and there was no growth in other areas of cargo preference shipping (such as intercoastal shipping) then between 350 and 475 jobs for sailors with U.S. citizenship or permanent residence would be lost.

However, there is growth in those other areas and so it is unlikely that impacts will be substantial. As indicated in the response to the issue of national security, the main impact on U.S. shipping of food aid cargo preference coupled with required U.S. sourcing of food aid is to enable U.S.-based shipping companies (40 percent of which are owned by foreign conglomerates) to keep old and inefficient ships in service. Effectively, food aid cargo preference is a form of corporate welfare that does nothing to enhance the competitiveness of U.S.-flag ships in international shipping markets.

Question. I understand that USAID and USDA are implementing similar non-emergency food aid programs in common geographic areas.

♦ How are the two agencies increasing and improving program coordination—in Washington and in the field—in order to reduce overlap and duplication with our limited resources for food assistance?

Answer. This is not my area of expertise. However, a recent GAO report has indicated that there is a need for more effective communication between the two agencies to achieve efficiency gains in coordination. However, I would defer to Dr. Mercier's expertize with respect to the issue of mission overlap between the two agencies. The programs they manage do have clearly defined mandates that are distinct and rarely target exactly the same problems.

Question. I understand that before I came to the Senate, last year's Farm Bill included reforms to allow increased flexibility for using a mix of U.S. commodities as well as locally and regionally procured (LRP) commodities.

♦ How much flexibility is currently allowed?

Answer. Under the 2014 Farm Bill provisions, the amount of funding allowed for local and regional souring was increased from $40 million a year (the amount allowed in the 2008 Farm Bill pilot program) to $80 million under the Food for Peace program, which is funded at a total of about $1.3 billion. That is about 6.15 percent of the total.

♦ Can you discuss the impact of this new flexibility on food aid?

Answer. The data indicate that every dollar spent through local and regional sourcing reduces the cost of delivering a ton of food to the target populations by about 40 percent. The reason the Senate Agricultural Committee strongly supported expansion of funding for local and regional sourcing in 2014 was precisely because the pilot program had been successful in enabling USAID to use efficient markets efficiently.

RESPONSES OF DR. STEPHANIE MERCIER TO QUESTIONS
SUBMITTED BY SENATOR DAVID PERDUE

Question. Coming to the Senate from the business sector, I appreciate your recommendations for increasing the efficiency of U.S. food aid to get more out of U.S. taxpayer dollars. I have heard from other sectors that these reforms might impact their industry.

Could you please speak to the impact of food aid reforms on the following sectors:

♦ U.S. agriculture;
♦ U.S. jobs in our ports;
♦ U.S. national security; and
♦ U.S. shipping?

Answer. *Impact on U.S. agriculture:* As I indicated in my written testimony, in recent years, the value of U.S. commodities exported under food aid programs accounts for less than 1 percent of total U.S. agricultural exports.

The share of food aid in overall exports varies somewhat among the commodity categories utilized for the programs, higher among certain processed commodities such as vegetable oil or blended products such as corn-soybean blend (CSB), and lower for bulk commodities such as corn and wheat. It is the former types of food that are most likely to see continued use if the Food for Peace program were to be provided with additional flexibility, as highly processed commodities produced in the United States were shown in the LRP pilot program to be more cost-competitive with similar categories of domestically produced commodities in developing countries. In addition, these products are most commonly used for direct feeding purposes in emergency assistance situations, which in many instances will require U.S.-sourced commodities because of food shortages in the recipient country.

As to the bulk commodities, these commodities are heavily traded on international markets, and any U.S. wheat or corn that is not sold for food aid purposes will find an outlet somewhere else in the commercial market. Although the commodity volumes in question are tiny as a share of international trade, if those resources are used more efficiently to purchase wheat or corn in developing country markets instead, to the extent that there is any price impact from these changes it would be a positive one, although likely modest at best.

Impact on U.S. port jobs: The data indicate that U.S. food aid shipments amount to well less than 1 percent of annual activity in most major U.S. ports. As described above, the commodities no longer shipped as food aid will eventually find other markets, many of them overseas, so the net impact on port activity from more extensive food aid reform would likely be close to zero. In addition, overall U.S. port activity across all categories of exports and imports has been climbing steadily in recent years, so any net change would be a shrinking share of total port business.

Impact on U.S. national security: USAID has estimated that the full flexibility of the Food for Peace program could allow the Agency to reach an additional 12 million beneficiaries annually as compared to the current impact of the program. Fewer hungry and consequently desperate people around the world with the expanded number of beneficiaries having good reason to be grateful for U.S. assistance, cannot be anything but a net positive for U.S. national security.

While the cargo preference program was nominally put into place to ensure that the U.S. military would have access to ample sea-lift capacity in the event of an emergency, the majority of U.S.-flagged vessels that carry food aid under those rules do not qualify for the Maritime Security Program and are not deemed to be militarily useful under the program's criteria. A 1994 GAO report entitled "Cargo Preference Requirements: Objectives Not Significantly Advanced When Used in U.S. Food Aid Program" raised significant concerns about this matter, as have other reports in recent years.

Impact on U.S. shipping: In general, U.S. export promotion programs are put in place to help U.S. firms level the playing field with other exporters in overseas markets. For example, the GSM–102 export credit guarantee program operated by USDA is designed to offset the advantage that European or Australian exporters receive by dint of their credit costs being lower because they are backed by their respective governments. In all other respects, U.S. agricultural exporters operate as efficiently as possible so as to be able to compete with other exporters on the open world markets for their commodities.

On the other hand, the cargo preference program essentially sets aside market share for U.S.-flag vessels to carry U.S. food aid, relieving them of the need to operate efficiently in that market so as to compete for that business. For the vessels included in the Maritime Security Program, data analyzed as part of a food aid project conducted at George Mason University indicate that food aid shipments are only a small part of their business, which could be easily replaced by military cargo (also covered under cargo preference rules) or other commercial cargo.

However, of the eight U.S.-flag vessels which carried the equivalent in tonnage of at least two complete shiploads of U.S. food aid between FY 2011–2013, it appears that none of them were registered under the Maritime Security Program during that period. In fact, the two companies which carried 62 percent of the U.S. food aid tonnage shipped during this period under the preference program had no MSP vessels carrying U.S. food aid at all. A 2011 study by the U.S. Maritime Administration (MARAD) found that the average U.S.-flag vessels had operating costs 2.7 times higher than comparable foreign-flag vessels. A portion of the difference is due to more stringent wage and environmental rules faced by U.S. carriers, but part of the difference is due to the greater age and cost inefficiencies of the vessels themselves.

The evidence suggests that in the absence of cargo preference rules, which essentially creates a guaranteed market for the services of these ships, these older non-MSP ships with their higher cost/pricing structure could not be operated on a profitable basis if faced with open competition. In a Department of Defense letter in 2013, it was estimated that food aid reform could affect the jobs of up to 495 mariners, or less than 2 percent of members of the merchant marine as classified in the Bureau of Labor Statistics data. However, since the volume of goods carried in traffic between U.S. states has been increasing steadily in recent years, it is likely that most of those mariners could easily find new jobs on those ships.

Question. I understand that USAID and USDA are implementing similar non-emergency food aid programs in common geographic areas.

♦ How are the two agencies increasing and improving program coordination—in Washington and in the field—in order to reduce overlap and duplication with our limited resources for food assistance?

Answer. In FY13, there were 8 countries in which both Food for Peace non-emergency projects and Food for Progress projects were underway, out of a total of 43 countries where projects were ongoing under both programs. These countries were Bangladesh, Burkina Faso, Ethiopia, Guatemala, Liberia, Malawi, Mali, Mauritania, Mozambique, and Uganda. While both programs operate in each of these countries, they often work in different parts of the countries targeting different populations.

For example, there are two Food for Progress projects going on in Uganda, one run by Mercy Corps and the other by the National Cooperative Business Association (NCBA). Both of these projects are operating in northern Uganda, which is still recovering from a decades-long civil conflict with the group the Lord's Resistance Army (LRA), which drove hundreds of thousands of Ugandans from their homes. There is also a title II development project going on in Uganda, run by the cooperative ACDI–VOCA. This project is targeted at the Karamoja region, which is in the northeast corner of the country.

On the ground USG coordination and oversight of these programs run by USDA and USAID is probably hampered by recent actions by FAS to reduce the number of attaché offices it operates overseas due to budget pressures. Of the eight countries listed above, there are attaché offices in-country in only two of them: Guatemala and Ethiopia. In the other six countries, there are at most locally employed staff working on agricultural issues in the U.S. Embassy (i.e., not U.S. nationals); otherwise agricultural issues are being monitored by FAS staff in a neighboring country's capital, such as the FAS office in Nairobi, Kenya, also has responsibility for agriculture in Uganda.

Nonetheless, the various U.S. Government agencies involved in overseas development assistance are doing a much better job of coordinating their activities than was the case just a few years ago. With respect to Uganda again, there is an extensive set of documents available on the USAID Web site which describes all the U.S. Government activities currently being conducted in the Karamoja region and how they are being integrated. Recognizing that coordination is a challenge, the Global Food Security Act reported out of the House Foreign Affairs Committee on April 23 seeks to create a stronger interagency mechanism to ensure cooperation and a coherent approach between U.S. agencies with programming or expertise in agriculture development/food security.

Question. I understand that before I came to the Senate, last year's farm bill included reforms to allow increased flexibility for using a mix of U.S. commodities as well as locally and regionally procured (LRP) commodities.

♦ How much flexibility is currently allowed?
♦ Can you discuss the impact of this new flexibility on food aid?

Answer. The legislative authority for the Food for Peace program has a specific section (section 202(e)) which allows implementing partners to request a specified share of the resources they are provided to undertake their projects as cash to cover nonfood expenses. As established under the 2008 farm bill, the maximum percentage allowed under the law was 13 percent. In the 2014 farm bill, that maximum was raised to 20 percent, and the category of expenses that could be covered with these resources was expanded. In effect, the share of title II resources that can now be used flexibly was increased by 7 percentage points. Most of this increased flexibility was used to provide PVO's operating nonemergency, development projects under title II with the ability to forgo using monetization transactions (selling U.S. commodities in local markets and use the proceeds to cover nonfood expenses). This change eliminates the inefficiency of converting commodities into cash which wasted at least 25 cents of every dollar spent on U.S. food aid for these projects, allowing the PVO's to actually reach an additional 600,000 people annually. Some monetization still occurs under title II because the provision requiring minimum monetization of at least 15 percent remains in law, but otherwise monetization only occurs when it makes sense as part of the development activity, not just to generate cash.

In addition, the 2014 farm bill established a new stand-alone authority for USDA to run a local and regional procurement program (LRP), authorized to spend up to $80 million annually. This authority can be used to acquire local foods to complement U.S.-sourced commodities used in school feeding programs under the McGovern-Dole program, or to quickly respond to small-scale emergency situations. This program received no appropriation for FY15 so is not currently being operated, but the President's FY16 budget request did include $20 million for this new program.

RESPONSES OF DAVID RAY TO QUESTIONS
SUBMITTED BY SENATOR DAVID PERDUE

Question. Coming to the Senate from the business sector, I appreciate your recommendations for increasing the efficiency of U.S. food aid to get more out of U.S. taxpayer dollars. I have heard from other sectors that these reforms might impact their industry. Could you please speak to the impact of food aid reforms on the following sectors:

◆ U.S. Agriculture?

Answer. Food aid programs in recent years have accounted for less than 1 percent of total U.S. agricultural exports. Therefore reforming food aid will likely have minimal impact on U.S. agriculture as a whole. It is also important to keep in mind that reforming food aid does not mean entirely abandoning use of U.S. commodities, only increasing flexibility to use the most cost efficient and appropriate method according to the context. There is always be a need for U.S. commodity in order to meet nutritional needs of specific target groups (lactating women and children under 2 years of age), or when markets cannot function and/or nutritionally appropriate food is not available. Likewise, certain processed commodities will likely continue to be primarily sourced from the United States, such as vegetable oil, because it is more cost effective. Food aid makes up a negligible amount of other bulk commodities that are already largely traded on the international market, such as a wheat and corn. Procuring less of these commodities for food aid purposes is unlikely to negative impacts and additional market outlets will continue to make up the majority of the market.

Again, it is worth noting that any commodity currently used for food aid can still play a role in providing this assistance overseas. Circumstances where food is not locally or regionally available, or when it is more cost efficient and timely to use U.S. commodities, such as some places in Latin America, will still involve U.S. agriculture. Reform is unlikely to have negative impacts on U.S. agricultural markets and will mean flexibility to provide more efficient and lifesaving assistance worldwide.

◆ U.S. Jobs in Our Ports?

Answer. U.S. food aid shipments make up a minimal amount of activity in most major U.S. ports, less than 1 percent annually. Port workers are often paid by the tonnage loaded, and flexible food aid funding could increase cost-efficiency in the program, thus allowing for more U.S.-made prepackaged goods to be purchased and then loaded by dock workers. It is also critical to note the overall U.S. port activity in both imports and exports has been steadily increasing in recent years. Due to this increase, there is demand for mariners and those involved in shipping food aid will likely have alternate shipping opportunities.

◆ U.S. National Security?

Answer. Reforming food aid can have a positive impact on U.S. national security. USAID has estimated as many as 12 million more beneficiaries can be reached annually if full flexibility is allowed for Food for Peace. This additional reach is badly needed as ISIS and other extremists continue to use food as an incentive and refugee numbers continue to rise. More people reached by U.S. food aid means less people desperate for food resources from other sources; this can only help the U.S.'s standing in the world and ultimately national security.

In terms of the cargo preference program, which meant to ensure the U.S. military will have enough sea-lift capacity in times of emergency through the Maritime Security Program, most U.S. flagged vessels carrying food aid do not qualify. Independent studies and GAO reports have found that because most vessels shipping food aid are not capable of being used for military purpose, reforms to food aid will not negatively impact the readiness of the U.S. military or national security. It is also important to point out that programs, such as the Department of Defense's Voluntary Intermodal Sealift Agreements (VISA) provide the U.S. military with significant additional sea power through Vessel Sharing Agreements (VSA) with both U.S. and non-U.S. flag ships. The Maritime Security Program ships are generally only activated once all preexisting VSAs and accelerated VSAs with both U.S. flag and foreign flag ships have been exhausted.

◆ U.S. Shipping?

Answer. The impact food aid reform will have on overall U.S. shipping is minimal. Currently there are U.S. export promotion programs helping U.S.-flag vessels to compete in the international market. However, because food aid cargo preference limits market competition, there are some U.S.-flag vessels carrying U.S. food aid that are able to continuously operate despite significant inefficiency. A 2011 study found that the average U.S.-flag vessel had an operating cost of 2.7 times higher than comparable foreign flag vessels, in large part because of the vessels were older.

In terms of the Maritime Security Program very few ships actually carrying food aid qualify for the program because of either the type of ship, age, or other inefficiencies. In addition, the Jones Act provides significant support to U.S. shipping as it requires that all goods transported by water between U.S. ports must be carried on U.S.-flag ships that are constructed in the United States, owned by U.S. citizens, and crewed by U.S. citizens and U.S. permanent residents. In addition, because of steadily increasing imports and exports across categories, mariners currently or previously involved in food aid shipments are not likely to be impacted by reforms. Additionally, it is important to recognize while food aid reform is unlikely to substantially impact the shipping industry, it will impact millions of additional beneficiaries worldwide through providing lifesaving assistance in a more cost and time efficient manner.

Question. I understand that USAID and USDA are implementing similar non-emergency food aid programs in common geographic areas.

♦ How are the two agencies increasing and improving program coordination—in Washington and in the field—in order to reduce overlap and duplication with our limited resources for food assistance?

Answer. Although there are USAID and USDA programs overlapping in 8 countries, it is CARE's understanding that these programs work with different populations in different areas. Budget constraints have meant difficulties in program coordination and oversight, particularly in the field. The Global Food Security Act (S. 1252/H.R. 1567), which focuses not on food aid but on long-term food security programs, recognizes issues in interagency coordination and provides mechanisms to further cooperation and develop integrated approaches between these agencies and their programs.

Question. I understand that before I came to the Senate, last year's farm bill included reforms to allow increased flexibility for using a mix of U.S. commodities as well as locally and regionally procured (LRP) commodities.

♦ How much flexibility is currently allowed?

Answer. PVOs are able to request a share of resources for project implementation as cash through Section 202(e) of the legislative authority for the Food for Peace program. The 2014 farm bill increased the maximum percentage from 13 percent to 20 percent and expanded the resources and activities covered by the account. In addition, the FY 2014 Omnibus provided an additional $35m on top of this 20-percent increase for 202(e) activities. These funding increases and the definition of expanded activities gives organizations implementing nonemergency title II projects flexibility to use alternate methods, such as local and regional procurement of food, and to forego monetization to some extent.

Monetization is the practice of selling U.S. commodities on local markets and using proceeds to fund development projects, however approximately 25 cents on every dollar is lost in this transaction. Monetization can also hurt local markets by flooding them with low priced U.S. commodities, negatively impacting the very people targeted by programs as beneficiaries. Current law requires 15 percent of title II funds to be used for monetization. However, increased flexibility in 202(e) has been helpful in offsetting monetization allowing 600,000 additional beneficiaries to be reached annually. It is important to note that the $35m in additional 202(e) funding provided through the FY14 Omnibus was limited to 1 year, and as such monetization activities are set to expand in future programs as this funding is no longer available to offset monetized activities.

♦ Can you discuss the impact of this new flexibility on food aid?

Answer. The impact of this flexibility is more cost efficient food aid for more beneficiaries, meaning additional lives saved and community served with more appropriate and sustainable mechanisms. Flexibility gives implementing PVOs the ability to use the most appropriate form of food aid, whether U.S. commodities, locally and regionally procuring foods, providing vouchers in functioning markets or some combination, depending on the context. Flexibility also ensures that U.S. food aid does not harm local markets through monetization, and can actually help build markets and effectively end long term dependence on food aid.

CARE's Kore Lavi program in Haiti program is an example of how flexibility in a Food for Peace program being implemented is already making positive impacts and sustainable outcomes. The program is designed and run in coordination with the Haitian Government, functions with high levels of oversight and accountability, and targets the poorest 10 percent of Haiti's population. Electronic vouchers can be used to buy staple foods, such as rice, and paper vouchers used to buy fresh foods, such as fruit and vegetables. The program emphasizes purchasing locally produced foods, helping to build the local market and supporting livelihoods of those living in the communities. Kore Lavi is in its second year, and so far the program has reached approximately 125,000 chronically hungry individuals and has partnered with 387 vendors, many of whom are women and other disenfranchised populations.

Kore Lavi is an example of a Food for Peace funded program using a combination of vouchers to purchase locally produced food, and in-kind U.S. food aid to supply additional nutrition to pregnant and lactating mothers.

Different communities have different needs, flexibility allows PVOs to best meet the needs of the beneficiaries and make the best use of tax payer dollars. The ability to not only provide food aid, but do it in a way that builds the capacities of local partners and beneficiaries links aid to resilient communities who are ultimately able to feed themselves and is made possible through increased flexibilty.